The Soul-Mate M... S0-BCG-676

A great resource for your relationship
and a superb way to help others with theirs

"David and Lisa provide tested and trusted insights that will help any marriage better honor God and experience all the joy and fulfillment He intended when He first came up with the idea back in the Garden."

—**Dr. Larry Osborne,**
bestselling author; conference and seminar speaker;
senior pastor, North Coast Church, Vista, California

"David and Lisa have found the marital missing link. Refreshing, practical, honest—a big thumbs-up for those who minister to couples and for couples in ministry!"

—**Alan Nelson,**
Executive Editor, *Rev! Magazine*

"We've watched and respected David and Lisa's marriage for many years. David delivered our wedding sermon over three years ago and we still talk about it to this day. We suspect that reading this book will provide you with a similar experience."

—**Christopher and Julie Rice**

"David and Lisa Frisbie are experienced, effective, and passionate marriage enrichment leaders. They not only write well about marriage; they live marriage well. Their insight is hewn from the rock of good practice. I highly endorse this wonderful new resource."

—**Jess Middendorf,**
General Superintendent, Church of the Nazarene

"I have known the Frisbies for more than 30 years, and they are the most authentic, clear-headed communicators of God's truth you'll ever encounter. They know it and they live it."

—**Dr. Dean Nelson,**
Director, Journalism Program, Point Loma Nazarene University

"I love hearing the Frisbies speak. They are hilarious, heart-warming, and real. Their books are like that too. But I think the secret of their success is their marriage itself: It is the closest, deepest, strongest, happiest marriage I have ever seen. They have the marriage all the rest of us want."

—**Doug and Lori Fisher**

"Everywhere I turn, pastors, ministry leaders, and business executives alike are working to navigate the challenges of a complex world. In the process, marriages are taking a huge toll. David and Lisa Frisbie are doing something about it. Their ministry is helping the rest of us get beyond survival to discover marriage that thrives on the deepest levels."

—Gary Mayes,
Vice president of Church Resource Ministries

"As society continues its relentless assault on marriage, the Frisbies have responded with a positive way through."

Dr. Paul G. Cunningham,
General Superintendent, Church of the Nazarene

"David and Lisa Frisbie speak from a wisdom they personally experience and have guided others into over many years…My marriage is thriving instead of broken due to their willingness to let God use them to provide answers and encouragement."

—Daniel MacEwan

"David and Lisa Frisbie know about marriage. They live out a beautiful love relationship every day that comes alive in their writing and their ministry."

—Dr. Hardy Weathers,
President and CEO of Nazarene Publishing House

"Married couples could have no greater allies than David and Lisa Frisbie. Their writing has helped untold couples confront and overcome issues that would keep their marriages from being all they can be."

—Larry Morris,
Adult Ministries Director, Sunday School and
Discipleship Ministries International,
Church of the Nazarene

"Dr. and Mrs. Frisbie have had a profound impact on my life…Our family has grown closer to the Lord through their teaching and Christlike example of living. We heartily endorse them as servants of Christ, and as gifted and experienced ministers of His truth!"

Mr. and Mrs. Nate Petty

The SOUL-MATE *Marriage*

DAVID & LISA FRISBIE

HARVEST HOUSE PUBLISHERS

EUGENE, OREGON

Cover by Koechel Peterson & Associates, Inc., Minneapolis, Minnesota

Cover photo © jerryhat/iStockphoto; back-cover author photos © Picture People

---

Statement About Privacy and Identification

Persons and couples appear in this book in one of two ways:

Where persons or couples are mentioned using *both* first and last names, these persons or couples are either public figures or have consented in writing that we may tell their stories, identifying them and/or quoting them by name. We are grateful to those who have not only told us their stories, but have also allowed us to identify them.

Where persons or couples are mentioned using first names only, certain key details of the story (including but not limited to names, location, marital status, number and sex of children) have been altered to prevent identification of the subjects while retaining the integrity and nature of the narrative. Therefore, with regard to first-name-only stories, any resemblance to any person of the same name, or in the same location, or in a similar situation, is entirely coincidental.

THE SOUL-MATE MARRIAGE
Copyright © 2008 by David and Lisa Frisbie
Published by Harvest House Publishers
Eugene, Oregon 97402
www.harvesthousepublishers.com

Library of Congress Cataloging-in-Publication Data
   Frisbie, David, 1955-
   The soul-mate marriage / David and Lisa Frisbie.
      p. cm.
   ISBN 978-0-7369-2245-6 (pbk.)
   1. Marriage—Religious aspects—Christianity. 2. Mate selection—Religious aspects—
Christianity. 3. Soul mates. I. Frisbie, Lisa, 1956- II. Title.
   BV835.F735 2008
   248.8'44—dc22

                                    2008020676

Printed in the United States of America

09 10 11 12 13 14 15 16 / VP-SK / 11 10 9 8 7 6 5 4 3 2

This book is for Chad and Rachel, who were married in a beautiful suburban Minneapolis home surrounded by their family and friends on an absolutely perfect day. This book is for Michael and Alice, who were united in marriage on an island out in the boundary waters between the U.S. and Canada, which we all reached by boat during a dazzling thunderstorm. It's for John and Sandra, who were married in a stone chapel with no electricity, built around the year 1200 on a windy hillside near a village in rural Switzerland.

This book is for all three of these loving couples, plus hundreds of others who have invited us to perform their wedding ceremonies around the globe. These couples have done more than invite us to officiate—they've taken us into their family circles and included us as cherished friends. We've learned from them as we've laughed and cried, counseled and listened, and prayed together seeking God's direction and His blessing.

This book is for Lonnie and Tasha, Naomi and Kevin, Ben and Missy, and Mindy and Darin. This book is for Blake and Eve, Barb and Miles, Barry and Pam, and Emily and Nate. It's for Tom and Sara, Bethany and Michael, and Taylor and Rob. It's for George and Kara, Jon and DeAnna, Linda and Alex. It's for Melissa and Trent, Chris and Julie, and Cathy and Dan. It's for Matt and Jennifer, Darren and Shelley, and Bob and Crissa. It's for Sara and Aaron, Jefry and Laurie, and Stephen and Nici.

This book is for Donnie and Bev, Bill and Rosa, Rory and Cathy, Tom and Tam, Steve and Tiffany, Percy and Mary, Bonnie and Rich, Scott and Tina, Bethany and David. It's for more than 300 of you so far. We apologize for not being able to list all of your names here in the dedication—all of you matter to us!

Thank you for including us as your journey of marriage began. Beyond that gift, thank you for welcoming us into your homes and also your hearts. After teaching people about marriage across the globe and for more than two decades, we are still learning…we're learning from you.

Contents

～

A Love for All Time   9

Part One: en/rapture

Chapter One　Chasing the Magic 15

Isn't there more than this? ～ T is for transparency ～
V is for vulnerability ～ The virtue of neutral friends
and guides

Part Two: de/construction

Chapter Two　Melting the Masks 45

The great pretender: how rare? ～ The absentee heart:
when a partner wanders ～ A hidden self: addictions
and self-destruction ～ Owning up to the mask: explor-
ing the disconnect ～ Courtship and marriage: too
often, the masks are still in place

Chapter Three　Crumbling the Walls 71

Same address, separate lives ～ Separation grows when
we don't deal with it ～ The walls must come down
～ Walls have two sides ～ Crumbling the walls calls
for more TV

Chapter Four　Busting the Ghosts 97

The sexual landscape of today's culture ～ Thoughts
happen: here's what to do about them ～ Ghosts in the
bedroom: passionate pictures ～ Working with God's
design, not against it

Chapter Five   Dying to Self 119

Where did this come from? This isn't who I am! ⌒
Humble servants and servant leaders ⌒ *Dying to self:*
a brief instruction manual ⌒ *Changing our lifelong*
patterns

Part Three: re/creation

Chapter Six   Birthing the Real 143

Setting the backdrop ⌒ *Growing up: the work we all*
must do ⌒ *Friends don't let friends remain immature*
⌒ *Maturity and immaturity: it's in the environment*

Chapter Seven Learning the Dance 163

Tales from the journey of denial ⌒ *Saying the difficult*
word "no" ⌒ *Newlyweds for life*

Chapter Eight Living the Love 183

How to move from pretty good to great ⌒ *Taking the*
time ⌒ *Two joys that come together and connect*

More help for the journey

Your TV Guide 201

Ideas for channeling greater transparency in your
marriage

Guide for Thought and Discussion 211

Questions to help you discover more about your relation-
ship and take action to move forward

Acknowledgments 219
Resources for Growth in Your Marriage 223

A Love for All Time

We all want the same thing, really.

What we want is Tom Hanks leaving his sleepless life in Seattle, flying across the country, running through traffic to find and save his little boy, racing to the top of the Empire State Building. He gets up there, throws his arms around his missing son, cries a little...then finds something he didn't believe was possible: the love of his life. She is waiting for him there.

Everything comes together for both of them in that one moment. He stares at her, she looks at him, they don't even speak. It's magic! Their hands reach out tentatively and find each other, then the newly formed couple walks slowly toward the elevator. The camera pans out. Cue the music: Forever begins here, and we know it's going to be fine.

This is what we want: Tom and Meg holding hands, just looking at each other. The movie can leave us there. Nothing more needs to be spelled out for us—we just know. These two will be fine, they'll last for all time, they'll be that one amazing marriage out of many millions. We know it without a word being spoken. These two are soul mates.

This is what we want: even though our parents didn't have it, even though our friends' parents didn't have it either, even though we've almost never seen it in real life, only in the movies. We want it because we know, in some silent place we never explore—crushed down inside our most private hopes and dreams—that this is how true love is meant to be. It is supposed to last forever, and it is designed to take our breath away.

We want that. Meanwhile our friends keep getting divorced, just like their parents did in their generation. Our new stepfather keeps telling us that his ex-wife is criminally insane—he thinks that she should be locked up. Maybe he's right. Sometimes it seems as if virtually every marriage relationship that we see around us is broken and falling apart...and yet we still cry out for the real thing, the genuine article, the one marriage that actually works and becomes a lifelong partnership of caring, committed equals.

Dear God, how we want that, even when we doubt that such a thing is possible.

We toss and turn, wide awake, dreaming of a love like that.

We lie there mourning inside, clammy and sweating, anxious and wondering if we'll be all alone for eternity, whether we're married or not. We want a companionship that reaches down deeper than sex or romance or friendship and becomes the two-in-one that Paul talks about, pastors always prescribe, and so few seem to know how to actually live.

Is there any point to chasing such a dream, or should we settle for reality as it is—clunky relationships that start strong but finish in anger, the early love dwindling down to a few key arguments about who keeps the kids, who gets the stuff, who pays the debts?

Should we give up or should we go for it? Should we cherish our silly romantic notions and go on hoping to find a partner who will still make our hearts sing, 20 or 30 or 65 years from now, someone crazy enough to love us just like we are?

We wonder and we worry. We make some mistakes and learn from them. Other mistakes become lifestyles—we keep repeating these errors, over and over again. Eventually most of us just quit hoping for more. We give up and settle for a so-so relationship. Or maybe we choose to stay single and not even try for the impossible.

Let's face it, if a Tom-and-Meg romance is "magic," what are the odds that such powerful magic will happen for ordinary people like us? We aren't the ones out there rolling lucky sevens all night at Mandalay Bay. That would be Brad Pitt, George Clooney, or someone else on the movie screen. In real life our aging Toyota is trashed out with scratched-off lottery tickets that didn't win. In real life good luck happens to other people, not us. "You are not a winner—please play again" should be our epitaph, it seems.

But what if breathtaking relationships aren't about fate or call-in radio shows or cross-country flights to meet strangers? What if speed-dating and chat rooms and all those Internet surveys are distractions that often lead us in unhelpful directions?

What if those really rare take-your-breath-away loves are formed by deliberate, intentional, often difficult choices that two people make, one day at a time, and keep on making for as long as it takes? Maybe that cute older couple that makes it look so easy, so natural, and so automatic actually struggled like anything for their first 15 years before learning how to even put up with each other, let alone be deeply satisfied.

We don't need to give up our romantic notions so much as we need to believe in them more powerfully and decisively than ever, taking action steps that move us forward toward commitment, responsibility, and self-sacrifice. True love happens—most often it happens when two people work for it, sweat for it, pray for it, make mistakes, keep on trying, learn patience, and hang in there. Only in the movie theater does true love happen in 90 minutes. Here in real life it tends to take quite a bit longer.

Should we believe in true love? Yes! We should also believe in getting rid of our bad habits, letting go of our stubborn ideas about things, and unplugging from our entire self-involved life focus. We should believe in caring about someone else so fully that we really do make sacrifices to build health and happiness into that person's life. True love is about making one small step at a time until the difficult task of surrender is somehow overtaken by the magic. We are caught up in a newness we can see and touch, taste and feel…yet we can't fully explain it or describe the process.

Hard work is like that—it pays off.

Grace happens, and some of God's children who are far from grace look around and cry, "Aha! There it is: There's the magic." It's the only way they know to describe what they see when God invades a hard-working committed love with His divine energy. Don't blame other people for not understanding God's ways; they're doing the best they can.

Grace happens, and it happens to people like you. What you need right now is not to *quit* believing, but to *start* believing. What you hope for is out there waiting for you, and the time to start reaching for it is right this minute.

One day, may little children of all ages look at your marriage relationship and say to themselves, "Aha! There it is: There's the magic." When that day comes, you will know, and your partner will also know, that this so-called magic cost both of you blood and sweat and tears. Both of you will know that—somewhere in the midst of all your believing and working and praying and hoping, somewhere between the failing and the starting over, somewhere when you almost doubted and gave up—grace happened.

May there be many such graces that bless the difficult places of your marriage journey.

part one:

en/rapture

1

Chasing the Magic

*It's more difficult to look at marriage as we actually experience it,
taking note of its deep fantasies, its hidden emotions,
and its place in the life of the soul; not looking for perfection,
but asking what the soul is doing when it entices us
toward such a demanding form of relationship.*

—Thomas Moore

There's a wispy goatee on his chin, just a few strands of curly blondish hair, straggly and long. He reaches up every few minutes and plays with the hairs, curling them around his fingers, twisting and twirling and then smoothing them out again. For all I can tell, his goatee is the only thing in the world that truly fascinates him.

He's sitting directly across the desk from me, just a few feet away, but he avoids making eye contact. Instead, he occasionally seems interested in a montage of pictures on the wall behind my desk—photos of Lisa and me traveling through China with our daughter Julie. In one photo we are hiking upward along the Great Wall. Another shows us dining, cross-legged around a common table, in a small rural village. Looking past me Garrett stares at the pictures, clicking the top of his pen.

Click-click.

The young husband rubs his chin, stares at the picture on the wall, clicks his pen. So far he hasn't said much, though he blushed out a shy hello earlier as I welcomed him into my office. He seems to be the strong and silent type—big on staring and clicking.

Click-click. Click-click. Click-click.

The noise must drive his wife crazy, I think to myself. *Does he do this at home?* As a marriage and family counselor I am familiar with all manners of passive–aggressive behavior, but I've never seen pen-clicking used as a weapon of avoidance or payback.

His wife, seated beside him, seems not to notice. In this couple she is clearly the social one—warm and outgoing. She looks straight across the desk, directly into my eyes, making sure I'm paying attention to her. When she speaks her voice is clear and strong, cutting through the noise of the pen clicks.

"We're not here because of any problems" is Danielle's opening statement to me. "It's not that. We have a good marriage. We love each other and we both love our kids."

"We don't really know why we came to see you," she continues. "Except it just feels like there ought to be more than this, you know? I mean, is this what marriage is? You live together, one of you chases kids around all day, and one of you goes off to work and then comes home? You eat together and sleep together, and eventually you get old?"

She watches me, makes sure I understand this, checks to be quite certain of my agreement before proceeding further. She's dressed in upscale business casual today, a cream-colored oxford shirt tucked in over neatly pressed khakis. Her husband slouches in his chair, absently rubbing his goatee. He's wearing a wrinkled T-shirt over faded jeans. His sandals are old, tattered, wearing out at the straps and heels.

Opposites attract.

Leaning back in my seat I nod at the young wife, silently inviting her to continue with her story. After many years of practice my nod is a way of saying, *I'm listening; I'm very receptive to what you're telling me. I halfway agree with you so far, even though you're just beginning to open up. So please tell me more.*

Quite a lot of content for one nod. It's taken years to refine it.

The young wife sighs, interprets the nod correctly, and then plunges forward.

"It's just…" Danielle begins. She wrinkles her nose, showing a small dimple in her left cheek, clearly trying to find the just-right phrasing to express her many thoughts. "Well, it's just that both of us feel like we're not really connecting anymore. I mean we live together, and we're raising two children together, but most of the time I feel like we're complete strangers. It's like we don't even know each other.

"We almost never talk about anything meaningful, or go for long walks, or do anything romantic together. All we do is get up every morning and go through the same old motions. We don't scream or fight—I sometimes think it might be better if we did!"

Her husband glances up at me, sees me looking at him, and quickly looks away.

He strokes his goatee and clicks his pen.

Click-click. Click-click. Click-click.

I consider telling him to stop. Rethinking it, I decide to ignore the sound as if it couldn't possibly matter. I don't even hear it.

I sit quietly and gather my thoughts for a moment—waiting, listening. Then I look patiently at the wife, who is wrinkling her nose again and about to speak.

"We don't really know why we came to see you," she continues. "Except it just feels like there ought to be more than this, you know? I mean, is this what marriage is? You live together, one of you chases kids around all day, and one of you goes off to work and then comes home? You eat together and sleep together, and eventually you get old?"

She's not aware of it, but her voice has gotten louder. She's been leaning forward in her seat, almost making a speech. She is obviously passionate about this topic and is getting herself a little worked up. It's clear she's been thinking about these issues and wondering if there's more to life, or if she should just settle for an "ordinary" marriage—a marriage like the ones she sees all around her, including at church.

They must be about five years in, I think to myself. Two kids, all the normal parental challenges and adjustments going on, not much real intimacy or relational depth. I give them four years minimum, seven years maximum, probably five years.

"How long have you been married?" I ask the wrinkly-nosed wife.

"Almost six years," she sighs. "It will be six years this June."

I say nothing, absorbing her answer, letting the silence congeal for a moment. I give myself imaginary bonus points for guessing the duration of their marriage union, although truly it's not difficult. After a while the patterns emerge clearly and visibly.

Danielle's husband clicks his pen again, staring at the grouping of China photos. He seems to be wondering if there's any point at all to marriage counseling, any point to going through all of this. His body language tells me he thinks he's wasting his time—he'd rather not be here. Has he heard anything his wife has said to me? Was he even listening? It may be impossible to know, but it's definitely time to find out.

I look directly at him, smiling, waiting until he meets my gaze.

"What could be better about your marriage?" I ask him. "What needs improving?"

He gives me a wry, Bart Simpson grin. "More sex would be nice," he says.

His wife elbows him in the stomach, and immediately they start a fake fight.

They're punching and scratching at each other, halfheartedly, giggling. I get a glimpse of the relational glue that's held them together so far. It's encouraging to see. Marriages are a lot like paper airplanes or fragile kites—although they're meant to soar, the world is a windy and sometimes stormy place. A lot of kites crash. Too many planes start out aiming skyward but end up nose-down in the dirt, crumpled and broken.

Garrett and Dani love each other—it shows in their fake-fighting. She's punching him in the left shoulder and he's slapping at her, not really connecting, trying to ward her off and yet keep her fighting back at the same time. Both of them are laughing out loud.

If love is friendship on fire, it's nice to see a few sparks fly.

I let the silly fight play out for a few minutes. It seems to destress the husband. And his wife is enjoying the chance to slap him around a little. She scores a few good hits, probably because he allows it. I notice he is fighting carefully, not using much force. They don't seem angry at each other; they seem playful, competitive, and childlike.

They pause in mid-battle, both a little embarrassed but relaxed and happier also. It's good for them to be like this, young and crazy, fake-fighting. Mr. Strong-and-Silent has come alive in this exchange, and now he's trying to tickle his wife into submission.

It isn't working.

Laughing and fighting back, Danielle looks across the desk at me.

"You see?" she asks me, her voice smiling. "You see what I have to put up with?"

Isn't There More Than This?

Couples like Garrett and Dani walk through my office door almost every day. They arrive shy and uncertain, sit down in comfy chairs or nest together on a large overstuffed sofa, and begin the process of looking for answers. Very few of them can articulate what they're looking for. Words like *more* or *deeper* sprinkle their conversations with me. They're not particularly searching for more sex (okay, some are) but rather more meaning, more value, more connectedness.

They're trapped in the routine, but they're chasing the magic.

Is there more to it than this? they wonder. *Shouldn't marriage be a unifying journey that bonds two people in the deepest, most meaningful connection and love?*

They know what they want, but sometimes they've grown afraid to hope.

Couples like Garrett and Dani sign up for our "Marriage

Enrichment Weekends" and "Renewing Your Marriage" retreats and seminars we travel to speak at. They file into church basements and high school gymnasiums, into community centers and large metro hotel ballrooms.

Some of the couples who attend our seminars share a ministry as pastors, missionaries, or church leaders. Their points of contact and areas of commonality with other marriages cut sharply across and puncture the differences. Regardless of age, years married, geographic region, socioeconomic status, and many other variables, sooner or later every married couple gets around to the same goal: We want more.

When we first began speaking to married couples at weekend retreats and family conferences, we discovered something that deeply surprised us. We were amazed to learn that many couples end up attending marriage retreats and marriage conferences more than once. They are repeat visitors to this strange four- or five-session alchemy of doctoring a relationship toward better health in the space of a few quick hours.

Early in the opening session of a weekend seminar or family conference, we often throw out this question: "How many of you have attended at least one marriage retreat or marriage enrichment seminar before coming to this one?"

Almost always, somewhere between one-fourth and one-third of the audience raise their hands. We've had a few seminars in which it appeared that half the crowd had come with previous experience at marriage enrichment or marriage renewal retreats or seminars. It's always shocking to see how many people have tried this before and have decided to come back again. After all, how many times can you hear that you need to communicate better, or that you need to learn how to resolve your conflicts?

Let's face it, marriage retreats (which are wonderful things, we enjoy them) involve a nice mix of laughter, relaxation, as much socializing as you like, time away from the kids, and lessons about how to communicate better and how to fight fair. The curriculum for most of them—no matter who is teaching and what book they're selling—is pretty much the same. By the time you've attended three or four of these kinds of sessions—or presented forty or fifty of them—you already know the drill. Whether you're watching for clues on a Power-Point presentation, laughing at silly video clips, or filling in the blanks of a workbook, when it's all said and done the material is pretty much the same.

Fight fair. Communicate better. Go on date nights more often.

The messages are often the same, definitely repetitive. So why do couples keep coming back for more of this?

We ask them, and from one coast of North America to the other, they tell us. Across Europe and Asia, they say the same thing.

"There has to be more," couples tell us, especially those in their twenties and thirties. "We know our marriage can be better than this, but how? We're tired all the time, all we do is chase the kids around, go to work and come back, and try to survive till tomorrow."

Couples with infants and very young children are even more direct.

"I'm going crazy!" a young mom may tell us. Beside her, her husband often smiles or affirms the statement. Then we listen as one or both of them complain to us about late-night feedings, colic, childhood diseases, the baby's lack of interest in feeding—all of which are early parenting issues that are normal to life, but cause couples stress and uncertainty. Each couple seems to think they're unpacking a unique or special situation. Instead, after more than two decades of doing this professionally, we can proclaim with certainty that most marriages experience these same seasons and these same obstacles along the pathway to maturity, intimacy, and lasting love.

Would you find it hard to believe—some couples attend these events just to get away from their screaming kids for a while? Can you blame them? It's fairly easy to find a few weekend babysitters, particularly among your church friends and relatives, if you present a noble cause like going to a marriage enrichment retreat. People are glad to help, and if you belong to at least a medium-sized church you probably won't lack for volunteers to watch your kids while you get away to work on your relationship.

Grandparents, aunts and uncles, and married and single siblings may be more than ready to volunteer their services, especially if they believe they're helping you learn and grow as a couple.

Even empty-nesters are repeat visitors at our retreats. "We feel like we don't know each other anymore," they'll tell us. "Now that the kids are gone, we're finding that we don't have much in common. It's scary—maybe this is why so many couples break up even after a long time of being together."

One way or another, couples attending their second or fifth or ninth marriage renewal event tell us they're searching for something deeper and better, no matter what stage of life they're in or how old their children are. Couples without children come to marriage retreats too—the core issues of striving toward unity are at the heart of good marriage relationships in all seasons. These issues are not connected to family size, or age, or demographics of region, economic status, culture, or race.

Many couples come to one marriage retreat, then later come back for another one. They're searching for techniques or mechanics or steps or a program that will solve their deep yearning to be together as one—at the soul level, not just in zip code.

Like U2, they still haven't found what they're searching for. But greatly to their credit, at least they don't give up.

Thirty minutes after Garrett and Danielle arrive for their first counseling session, we are starting to make a little progress together. We've all gotten more comfortable—the couple's fake fight seems to have relaxed them. It's time for me to begin telling them what their relationship needs.

They're not prepared for the answer I give them.

What your marriage needs, I explain to them carefully, is...more TV.

Both of them stare at me like I've gone completely insane. *More TV?*

After a moment's pause, Garrett gives me a knowing nod, looking at me with an expression that seems to say, "Dude, this is such excellent advice!" He appears to believe I am advising him to get the full NFL package, every game all season long, plus the NBA and NHL full-season add-ons.

More TV?

Garrett is buying into this big-time. He likes counseling now. He's become a believer, and he's ready to champion my cause forever.

I ruin the moment by explaining to him what I mean.

In every chapter of this book, regardless of its title, regardless of the quotes at the start, regardless of everything else—we'll be looking together at the idea of more TV.

TV is the absolute key to understanding how relationships go from good to great, how close friendships or marriages or accountability groups or investment partnerships make the journey from just-hanging-out-together to we're-bonded-for-life greatness.

TV is an acronym for the two most important qualities you need in order to succeed.

So before we return to Garrett and Dani's journey, let's look at some TV.

T Is for Transparency

T is for transparency. You won't move an existing relationship to a deeper level until you're willing to let people see you as you are, for who you are, without pretending to be more cool, more smart, more together, more self-controlled, or more anything else than you really are. How many genuinely transparent people do you know? Go ahead and count them on your fingers. Don't worry about it: You won't need both hands.

When the container of a light source is transparent we can see right through it. By contrast, a container that is translucent lets much of the light shine through, but doesn't let us see what's inside it. That's a major difference. There are some things we may be able to see, while many other things remain hidden from our view.

Most of us, whether consciously or not, grow up making the choice to be translucent people. We are opaque and cloudy, presentable on the surface, yet the inside is shrouded in mystery. Light may flow out of us, but no one can see where it comes from.

If we are Christians, we may end up being a lot like those stained-glass windows you see in some churches. So beautiful—what a lovely picture of Christ—and the light shines right through it. But it isn't possible to see what's behind the glass. Who or what is back there, anyway? We can't tell. We can't see the inner truth behind the surface picture.

Transparency almost always lacks the outward beauty of a stained-glass window, because a transparent surface reveals the reality behind the outside layers and outer gloss. This kind of transparency as a personal trait probably isn't very attractive unless you happen to be beautiful in your real, inner life. It seems quite possible that Mother Teresa was beautiful in her transparency, or perhaps Henri Nouwen was beautiful in his. Mahatma Gandhi may have been beautiful in his transparency. This is only speculation on our part. Lisa and I did not have the privilege of meeting these people, though we did hear Henri Nouwen speak and we love his writing. These three people—you can probably name others—seem to have chosen a high level of personal transparency as a way of life, humbly serving others and doing effective work in a hurting world. Such lives are remarkable and rare, which is why we tend to notice them.

Transparency always attracts and holds our attention. It's rare and unusual.

Taking Transparency on the Road

Sometimes transparency chooses us, even when we don't voluntarily choose it. These occasions can be embarrassing. They can be highly useful. Sometimes they can be both.

I recently spoke at the thirtieth reunion of my university class. Lisa and I were scheduled at the homecoming banquet at the local

Hyatt Regency hotel. We were also doing a book signing and personal appearance at a large Christian bookstore in the same area, and I was speaking to the whole group at our class reunion.

We'd be seeing classmates from 30 years before, and obviously we wanted to look our very best. I'd be speaking from the platform. Needless to say we brought our best clothes, some of them brand-new, all of them dry-cleaned and ready for the big show. We were prepared.

God, the airlines, or simple fate had a better idea.

Our flight from San Diego to Minneapolis was greatly delayed before departure. We sat out there on the runway, tantalizingly near the beach but unable to deplane and splash around in the frothing surf. There were delays, mechanical issues, explanations, and more delays. Much later we were finally airborne, way behind schedule.

By the time we landed in Minneapolis, there were no more flights to Kansas City that night—on any airline. Because the reunion was an early-morning breakfast event, we couldn't accept the airline's kind offer of a free hotel night and a complimentary late dinner in Minnesota—we needed to be in Kansas City early the next day.

We didn't ride the shuttle, nor did we accept the airline's offer of travel vouchers. We kept talking to ticket and counter agents, explaining the problem. After several hours of fruitless but persistent appeals at the ticket counter, and with the much-needed help of two supervisors, we were eventually routed to Chicago on a very late flight, and from there on into Kansas City on another airline on an even later flight, arriving long after midnight at an airport that was essentially closed down.

Our plane landed safely in Kansas City, but our luggage did not.

Very few high-end clothing stores are open in Kansas City between the hours of three and six on a Saturday morning. I had basically two options: I could call in sick (which seemed attractive to me), or I could show up for the reunion and give my speech wearing the same very casual clothes I had traveled in the day before.

Did I mention that the university had just elected a new president we'd never met, and that he'd be attending our reunion breakfast while I spoke?

No pressure or anything.

I didn't call in sick.

Instead I showed up for breakfast, 30 years after graduating from college, wearing a faded old polo shirt, my well-worn khakis, and my oldest pair of casual shoes, all of which I'd worn all the day before during our "planes, trains, and automobiles" travel day. I stood out more than a little bit—most people were clearly dressed for success.

Lisa, always prepared, likes to travel in "business casual" attire. She looked stunning that day wearing the previous day's traveling clothes. I didn't look stylish or successful or professional or wise—a trick of the eye I had hoped to achieve by wearing my best suit, a power tie, and some well-shined Bostonians. Instead of seeming hip and savvy I looked like who I really am: a middle-aged guy with a receding hairline, going gray here and there, a guy who loves living in southern California and who enjoys dressing casually and comfortably as often as possible, especially while waiting in line at major airports and while schlepping his luggage onto shuttle buses outside the terminals.

We did our book-signing gig in the same clothes. I certainly didn't choose to be so transparent that weekend. After 30 years of scratching around for a career, I would have welcomed a chance to look better, seem better, and come off as more impressive than I really am. (Isn't that the point of these reunions?) But transparency invaded my space without waiting around for an invitation.

The result—amazingly—was that people not only welcomed and accepted Lisa and me, but immediately bonded and connected with us. They could identify with our true story of lost luggage and rerouted flights. They laughed as I recounted our many travel ordeals. Who knew? It's better to show up at a reunion as you really are, instead of showing up pretending to be younger, richer, wiser, or more beautiful than you really are.

The new president of the university, a very classy guy, invited us to join him at the head table for that night's banquet at the Hyatt Regency. Kind of like Mr. Drysdale inviting Jethro and Elly May to be his guests for a swank event at the Beverly Hills Hilton. We went, we sat at his table, and we formed a friendship with an amazing man who somehow ignored the poverty and inappropriateness of our attire. Our respect for him grew enormously.

V is for Vulnerability

The V in TV is for vulnerability. Vulnerability is about choosing to be weak instead of strong, open instead of closed, caring and feeling instead of remaining aloof. Rabbits and deer are vulnerable; porcupines and armadillos much less so.

We're born like rabbits and deer. We are defenseless and vulnerable, and this is why our birth parents or the other adults who raise us try to protect us and keep us safe. But one way or another as we emerge into real life, we begin forming relationships and we get hurt. We trust a friend who betrays our secrets, we fall for a first crush who then abandons us, or we get involved in a close relationship that crashes and burns, wounding us deeply.

One way or another many of us end up choosing to be more like porcupines or armadillos. We may interact with people, but now we've got our guard up for good. We're wearing the armor. We hide our true selves behind layers of sharp points and thick skin, hidden away behind protective devices meant to keep us from further pain.

This is especially true after we gain some "experience" with love and romance. Maybe as a teen girl we have a great relationship with our first love. Then he dumps us. Or maybe as a university-age guy we're dating this amazing girl who is so impressive—but it turns out she's also dating two or three other people at the same time. She's not ready to choose, or maybe she chooses someone else. One way or another we participate in dating and bonding and the rituals of romance, and we often end up getting hurt.

Hurt happens.

Many of us learn from that, but we draw the wrong conclusions. We learn that love hurts, and we conclude that caring deeply about someone only leads to pain and suffering. We conclude that the only way to be "safe" is to hide from relationships and not get too attached to people. The lesson isn't essentially wrong: Life does hurt. But the conclusions we rush toward are not always helpful and fruitful for us in our later development. And the armor we build around ourselves only keeps us from finding the very love we desperately want.

Sometimes our armor protects the wrong places.

As family counselors Lisa and I often work with young adults who have misplaced armor. Many of them sexually "hook up" with someone else—but they do not allow their sexual partner to really get to know them. Although they give away their bodies, they simultaneously lock away their hearts. The very notion of "hooking up" seems to imply lack of commitment, shunning meaningful connection, and avoiding personal vulnerability—while being intimate only in body.

Bent on protecting their emotions and thus their true selves, these teens and young adults fail to defend their physical selves. Many of them end up damaged and broken in their physical bodies and emotions, burdened by STDs, feelings of guilt and shame, and sometimes also by unwanted pregnancies. Their defenses are carefully constructed around the wrong places. And meanwhile they are open and vulnerable in places where they can experience disease and harm.

The contrast is striking: armor around their emotional selves, not their physical selves. These wounded-by-life young adults close off their inner emotions and feelings. They refuse to be hurt again. They're fine with casual promiscuity, frequent one-night stands, and shallow relationships. They refuse to let themselves care about their partners, believing if they don't care they can't get hurt again. They are like sexually active porcupines.

Why are many of today's teens and adults willing to be sexually open and vulnerable, yet not willing to be open, honest, and vulnerable emotionally and personally? The answer is, they believe sex can't or won't hurt them (they are wrong about this, medically and psychologically as well as spiritually), but they believe that caring about someone is only a pathway to personal pain, now or in the future.

Open bodies, closed hearts: Is this the path of wisdom? Giving away physical health and personal innocence, settling for shallow hookups when the Creator designed us for lifelong unions with interesting, intimate partners?

Regardless of your moral perspective or your place on the journey of faith, this is tragic for families and for society at large. Wise, well-adjusted adults building healthy relationships and forming healthy family units form the foundation of a culture that will endure and thrive. Shallow, immature adults hooking up with temporary sex partners bring discord, uncertainty, and ultimately more brokenness into a social system that is already overloaded with brokenness and sorrow.

A Word of Caution and Understanding About Vulnerability

Let's be clear about what we mean, and equally clear about what we don't mean.

As we already know, close friendships and marriages may not be places of safety. Instead they may be places of harm or danger, places where we might be genuinely hurt. We enter these places expecting our dreams to come true, our hopes to be realized, and our future to be bright. We may leave these places bitterly disappointed and wounded.

When we recommend in this book that you should be emotionally vulnerable in a marriage, we are not advocating exposing yourself to violence—emotional or physical—nor are we advising you to lower your personal barriers so that someone can abuse you or degrade you. This book is specifically intended for married couples who love each other, who are committed to each other for life, and who want to take their relationship upward to the next level, and then to many positive levels beyond that. Please be absolutely certain that you understand the context of this recommendation—context is everything. Vulnerability is best reserved for times and places where it is appropriate and safe.

Brienne Murk, musician and author, has written a very helpful book entitled *Eyes Wide Open.* In it, Brienne, who sings with the music group Myrrh, shows singles—especially teen and college-age women—how and why they should guard their hearts and put boundaries around their affections. She argues that sexual purity should be joined by emotional purity, that the unmarried should keep themselves free from dangerous emotional entanglements. It's a wise book, and we are glad to recommend it to those who are teens and older as they explore relationships and dating.

Clearly, emotional vulnerability is not wise in all situations. Yet as we join our lives with another in holy marriage, we are creating the kind of space and the type of place where emotional vulnerability is not only appropriate, it is functionally necessary. We will not make progress in knowing and being known, in growing together deeply and meaningfully, until we are willing to open up, take risks, and be vulnerable. Finding a life partner and beginning the process of meaningful intimacy leads to the strongest partnership on earth, that of husband and wife, lover and beloved.

And the pathway to strength in a marriage begins by admitting our weakness.

Vulnerability is wisely saved for some times and some situations, and is to be chosen only in some ways. In this book we are focused mostly on learning about how to make a godly marriage relationship grow, a committed union between a man and a woman who are partners on the journey of life. These two adults aren't just casual friends or temporary associates. Instead, they are joined together in the sight of God, as witnessed by friends and family, and are pledged to a lifelong journey lived side by side, not apart.

If you are forming a lifelong partnership with a committed spouse, and if you want a relationship that goes deeper and becomes stronger, choosing to be emotionally vulnerable is not only appropriate for you, it is also a necessary step in the evolution and progress of your relationship. You won't move forward without it.

Back in my office, Garrett and Danielle are starting to talk with each other, and I'm listening.

When counseling works effectively we all get comfortable being together in one room, and the walls between husband and wife start to crumble. Realizing this is a place of safety, each partner begins to risk talking more honestly about what's really going on in their relationship—or what isn't going on but should be.

Today a few minutes of fake-fighting and laughter is yielding to gentle but honest discussions about married life, having kids, and the changes most married couples encounter and experience. The issues we're talking about are normal, natural, and common to almost every married couple who chooses to have children in the early years.

Garrett and Danielle, who stumbled into this office wanting a closer relationship but not knowing how to get there, are no exception. Although every relationship is unique, it's amazing how similar our problems are in the first few years of a marriage. We think we're the first to explore this new territory, but in reality many others have been there. Quite a few are there at this moment, just like we are!

It's becoming clear to me that Danielle and Garrett have a good marriage—they really do love each other, down underneath their many surface frustrations. They really do hope for more satisfaction than they're experiencing. They want more closeness, more intimacy, more togetherness—they just don't know how to make it happen. They've tried a few things on their own, but without much in the way of results. Each of them is beginning to wonder inwardly, *So, is this all there is? Is there any point to trying to reach for more, or should we settle for less?*

In the midst of these questions, both Garrett and Danielle have a genuine faith in God—although they're honest enough to admit that personal spiritual growth is not really happening for either one of them right now. Mostly, they're trying to survive the years of late-night child feedings, diaper changes, and a young toddler tearing up the house and making messes everywhere. They're trying to grow together in spite of feeling more and more apart; they're trying to live up to their original hopes about married life.

As they face these issues, they don't have sex as much anymore (his perspective).

As they confront these challenges, they don't meaningfully connect and talk together at a deep personal level like they did at the beginning (her viewpoint).

Yet here's the good news, part one: Instead of simply settling for this kind of life, Garrett and Dani have decided to reach out and seek some counseling, trying to find some clues that might point them toward a happier union. In their case, the motivation for marriage counseling seems to come from both sides of the bed, not just from one partner.

The good news continues: They've taken action steps. They've hired someone to do child care, they've scheduled an appointment with me, and today they're trying on a new counselor for size, seeing if he fits. They're sitting in my office like two explorers, crossing a strange and unfamiliar land in search of buried treasure. Is there any gold hidden around here somewhere? How do we find it? Can we afford to take this journey? Are you (counselor) a reliable guide to this new terrain, or should we find someone else?

Improvement Isn't an Accident

I hear very similar questions from almost every married couple I counsel. Their core questions tend to be the important ones: Can we get to a deeper place, to a life that is meaningful and fulfilling, to the kind of connectedness and unity, lasting romance, and satisfaction that both of us always hoped for? Is that kind of intensity even possible for our marriage?

They're curious: If there really is a way forward, what does the pathway look like as a relationship moves toward genuine closeness and real depth? What are the markers along the journey toward an intimate and close relationship?

These couples are asking the right questions. Their search brings them to a logical and good place to start looking for helpful answers—a marriage retreat or the office of a marriage counselor or minister. But whether couples search for this kind of help with a pastor, a close friend, an older married couple that models a strong marriage, or a paid professional counselor—the important thing is that wise couples choose to "go for it" instead of settling for less.

Your marriage will not improve if left to itself. Your relationship will not grow deeper by accident, by chance, or without work. The exception—and it's not an exception you're likely to want—is that sometimes intense tragedy or enormous adversity can prove unifying for a couple, as they rally to face an unexpected and difficult battle.

Apart from that, in the midst of real life and normal situations, marriages and relationships tend to slide toward stagnation, indifference, and unfruitfulness. It can be useful to think of your marriage like your front yard. If you simply ignore it and live your life, weeds will grow in a hurry. But if you want lush, green grass that is soft and inviting underfoot, you're going to have to work at the job, pay attention to the results, and take a lot of action steps, some of which may be expensive.

A week or so later Garrett is talking—really talking—opening up and revealing the way he feels as a husband and father and person. Although I've already told him three times today he needs to talk directly to Dani and not to me, he seems to be a slow learner. He hasn't applied this strategy yet.

Today is our second session together. This time we plunge into the deep end of the pool right away. We don't waste much time in the shallow water.

"Sometimes," Garrett is saying softly, in a quieter voice than usual, "sometimes I feel like she loves the baby more than she loves me. It's like I've been totally replaced in the relationship—first by Kyle, now by Kelsey. I mean…I don't know any other way to say this…it just seems like Dani gives all her love to those two kids, and there isn't any room left in her world for me."

Danielle is extremely quiet, processing what she is hearing. I am grateful that she doesn't lash out with some kind of a denial or argument right now—many wives would. The office is suddenly so quiet that all three of us can hear a computer printer, one room away in the reception area, suddenly awaken and begin spitting out pages of copy.

Dani says nothing. There is a very loud silence in my office.

Garrett tugs at his goatee, swallowing, looking down at the floor.

"Garrett," I remind him gently, waiting until he looks up at me. "Remember to talk directly to Dani, not to me. Please go ahead and say the exact things you just said, but this time don't say them *about* Dani, say them *to* Dani."

"I can't," Garrett says so quietly I almost don't hear him. "I can't do that."

"Yes you can, honey," Dani urges him softly. "I think this is what we need."

She's right, but I have no idea if her husband is wise enough to follow her in the direction of transparency and vulnerability. When it matters, can Garrett do more TV?

He weighs the risks, then decides to open up a little more.

"When Kyle was born…" he says to his wife, his voice quiet, tentative and uncertain, "when Kyle was born it was like you moved me out of your life completely. There wasn't room for me anymore. I would come home and find you holding him, or feeding him, or whatever—it was like the two of you were complete, like you didn't need me for anything. I felt like I'd been replaced, like I didn't matter to you anymore."

The words are tumbling out of him quickly. Garrett seems nervous and afraid, like he shouldn't be saying this, like he's letting something loose in the office that will rear up and destroy us all. The fear in him is stark and tangible; we can all sense it.

Danielle, by an act of God's grace or imparted mercy, is staying silent. Whoever raised this woman did it well. There is wisdom in her, genuine wisdom. She knows when to simply listen, not talk back. She has turned her chair to face Garrett as he talks to her; now she reaches out and grabs one of his hands and brings it to her lap. She does these things instinctively, not contriving, but humble, listening, open.

"Go on," she says to her husband of five years. "I think this is helping us."

Garrett swallows, looks at her intently, and resumes talking.

"I didn't mind it so much at first," he tells his wife. "I mean, I was proud of you and proud of our son, and when I looked at you I just felt so…I don't know…like my life had meaning or purpose, like I had achieved something really worthwhile, maybe for the first time ever. It felt good, mostly."

The young man pauses and looks down at the floor.

"But after a while, I kind of felt like I'd been moved out of first place in your life and now I was in second place. And before I could really adjust to that, here comes Kelsey. She bumps Kyle out of first place—now he's in second, and I'm way back there in third. It's like you love Kelsey with all your heart and you smother her with all your affection, and then you love Kyle too, and you give him a whole lot of attention, and then maybe if there's anything left over after you care about both of them, you get around to me…"

Garrett stops speaking. His body language shows he fears he's gone too far, now he wants to quit, wants to apologize and come crawling back. He's messed up and he wants to make it right—if it's not too late, if he hasn't said something so terrible that there's no fixing it. Has his sudden confession blown the relationship apart beyond repair?

There's a little tear in the corner of Dani's left eye, but her husband doesn't see it. Danielle, for her part, isn't letting her emotions control her. I watch her as she carefully composes herself, keeping it together, waiting in case there is more her husband wants to say to her. She seems open and yet guarded at the same time, waiting.

Garrett is finished with his explanations—at least for right now. All three of us sit in silence for a little while. The computer printer in the outer office finishes its task and also falls silent. There is almost no noise in the room; we can all hear ourselves breathing.

"Wow," Garrett finally sighs after perhaps two or three minutes of silence. "I've never said any of this stuff out loud before. But to be honest, this is exactly how I've felt since right after Kyle was born. I mean..."

His voice trails off into empty space leaving his sentence unfinished.

Dani looks across the desk at me, wondering what comes next. Her eyes seem to be asking me, "Is it my turn to say something now, or what?"

The Virtue of Neutral Friends and Guides

An hour or so later our session is drawing to a close. Garrett and Dani have been talking with each other nearly nonstop, almost forgetting I'm here at times. Like many other couples of all ages, the two seem able to talk more freely here in this office, with a counselor present, than in the privacy of their own home.

It's one of the ongoing mysteries of the counseling process. Somehow having a neutral, benevolent (and hopefully prayerful) third party makes it easier to communicate. Maybe we're more careful in how we say things when an outsider is listening. Perhaps we're less likely to give in to anger, get sarcastic, or let off a blast of sudden criticism. It could be as simple as having a referee present to blow the whistle in case someone commits a foul during the big game. For whatever reason, a counselor's office often becomes a place of safety where we can take risks we might otherwise avoid.

My office is functioning that way today, as it frequently does, and I'm grateful.

Dani looks at me late in our session, her eyes reddened from some useful crying. "Can we do this a few more times?" she asks me. "Can we get together with you at this same time next Thursday night? Does that work for you?"

The DayTimer on my desk shows an open time slot for next Thursday evening. "I'm putting it on my calendar right now," I tell the young couple as they watch me write their names into my organizer. "Let's get together at the same time, next Thursday night."

Danielle reaches for a Kleenex from the box on my desk, pulls one out with a precise motion, dabs at her eyes. Always graceful, she folds the tissue into her pocket and looks directly at me.

"Thank you," she says to me. She doesn't mean for the Kleenex.

Garrett gives me a very probing look, this time actually seeing me and communicating with me person to person. "Man, we needed this," he says. "I can't believe how long I've been holding all this inside me. I can't believe how good it feels to finally get it out."

His wife hugs him, clings to him, leans into him and absorbs his strength.

After a closing prayer, the two of them leave my office. As they walk toward their car I'm indoors praying for them, watching them from my window, grateful for what their body language shows as they cross the parking lot. Dani leans her head over on Garrett's shoulder as they walk. Garrett appears to be talking to her. Extra points for the twentysomething husband—he actually opens the car door for his wife. A rare gentleman.

They'll drive home, relieve the babysitter for the night, and rejoin the chaos of life with two young kids soon enough. Before that, at my suggestion they're stopping along the way for some ice cream. I've given them directions to a nearby Coldstone Creamery.

Every doctor has to write a few prescriptions now and then.

A New Respect for Marriage

So far this particular week, Garrett and Dani are the third twentysomething couple who has stopped by for marriage counseling—and it's only Thursday night. I have quite a few more appointments listed for Friday and Saturday, so I thumb through my DayTimer and notice that two more twentysomething couples are scheduled to come in before Sunday, in addition to those from other age groups.

The majority of these couples come for counseling because their relationships are seriously missing out on TV. "Our sex life is great!" some of them tell me. "That's not the problem." As we explore the dynamics of their relationship together, it becomes clear that at least one of them has never learned how to be transparent; at least one of them has never chosen to take the risk of being fully vulnerable. Although it's most often the man who avoids emotional closeness, this unhelpful choice can be made by either sex.

By holding back from TV, these couples are missing the relational depth they say they want. They are chasing the magic, but the magic keeps running away from them. Why? It is so much easier to learn a technique than it is to quit pretending. It is so much simpler to keep your guard up than it is to let your walls crumble and to be known, loved, and celebrated for who you really are.

Unwilling to let go and be real, however, we keep on chasing the magic. Why then are we surprised when we don't catch it, when our relationship sours and fades, when we seem to lose the romance and love that once bloomed in our hearts and our lives?

In spite of what is commonly believed, marriage may not be more difficult now than it was before. Marriage has always been a challenge, for every generation. The difference, I think, is that couples today are more willing to seek counsel, more likely to admit they don't have their act together, more inclined to reach out and get help instead of suffering in silence and watching a good relationship slowly go sour. Quite a few twentysomethings grew up watching their baby-boomer parents split up and divorce. These same twentysomethings tend to believe their parents didn't try hard enough to work out their relational problems.

Today's young marrieds seem determined not to repeat those mistakes. Optimistic and willing to make sacrifices, they're more likely to ask their pastor or a close friend for some help. When things start going wrong, these couples begin to search for answers faster. And if for any reason they're not happy with the counseling they receive, they don't give up on counseling itself—they just find a new counselor to work with. They keep trying.

Raised in brokenness, today's husbands and wives are insisting there must be a better model than what they've seen. For the sake of their children, today's couples who choose to marry are determined to not only stay together but also share a learning, growing, always-improving relationship so that their children view marriage as desirable, fulfilling, and relevant. This is true outside the church doors as well as in the pews.

This current generation of couples is trying to make marriage work, and in some ways it is working: By many measures the divorce rate is in decline, and the downward trend seems to be consistent. Has the divorce rate passed its peak in our society never to climb so high again? Will the current trend continue in the future?

Although there are multiple causes of fewer divorces today, including the prevalence of couples living together without a formal and legal marriage agreement, we see plenty of evidence every day showing that today's couples choosing to marry are increasingly committed to the idea of staying together for life. Couples that do marry are beginning to move away from the idea of marriage as a temporary, disposable, "sure hope it works" arrangement. Despite the brokenness of our social networks across the landscape, marriage itself is regaining a respect that's been missing for a generation or more.

Given the high economic and social cost when a family unit dissolves, the federal government has gotten on board in the effort to strengthen marriages. States are passing laws requiring pre-marriage counseling, or they're offering discounted marriage licenses if couples are willing to enroll in some useful instruction before the wedding. These efforts are well-intended and have the potential to increase the viability of marriages while preventing unwise marriages from happening in the first place. (More on this later.)

Seeking Depth

Yet the rest of the story is that a successful marriage is not only about longevity, it's about passion and depth. The union we seek is not just quantitative (until death) but also qualitative (our best marriage now).

Accordingly, today's couples choosing to marry are looking for a quality of life that is deeper than just staying together under the same roof. These couples want a satisfying and enduring relationship, not just a chance to own a nice house and raise a few kids together.

They tend to want a lifelong love. Why should they settle for less? Why shouldn't they believe that closeness and intimacy are within reach as couples bond and connect for life?

Making a Comeback in Your Own Marriage

With ideas like covenant marriage, sacred marriage, and accountable marriage making headlines and shaping policy decisions, it's clear that the idea of marriage is being nourished and built up from many sources. What's true at the broader level deserves a chance to be true in your own union as well, where marriage plays out every day at the intimate level of your own experience and reality.

Whether you are 25 or 45, whether you're newly married or two decades along on your marriage journey, this book is written to help you move forward, finding a deeper level of intimacy with your partner than ever before. Maybe, like Garrett and Dani, you will be motivated to reach out for help when you need it. Go find a nearby church or a psychologist. Sit down with a marriage counselor, a rabbi, or your parish priest. Talk about what's going on in your relationship and make an honest effort to work it through.

Not happy with the counselor you find? Keep looking. Search the Internet, ask your married friends, try the counseling center at that new megachurch out by the highway. Keep looking until you find a counselor both of you are comfortable with.

Many insurance policies cover marriage and family counseling, and most agencies that offer counseling have a sliding scale that adjusts according to what you can afford. Don't stay away from counseling because you fear the expense. Pursue counseling because it has the potential to change your life for the better, beginning right now.

〰〰〰〰〰〰〰〰〰〰〰〰〰〰〰〰〰〰〰〰〰〰〰〰〰

⌒

The ideas and stories in these pages will help you learn about how relationships grow and change. Like many couples, you may be striving to take your marriage from good to great. If so, this book is written with you in mind. Consider these pages a road map for the journey to excellence. (Skip around if you want to. You don't need to read the chapters in numerical order.)

Take the chance to learn from the examples and illustrations that are drawn from real life. Do you find a marriage here that is much like your own? Do you see parallels with your own relationship and your own emotional or spiritual journey? What are you discovering as you read these chapters? What did you already know, and what is brand-new to you?

Wherever you are on your marriage journey, there are hints, tips, ideas, and strategies in this book that can change your relationship forever, making it deeper and stronger than you ever dared to hope for. But be warned up front: There aren't any shortcuts. Growing deeper is not about following an outline or learning a new skill; a meaningful union is rooted in becoming honest and open, weak and real.

In the next part we'll look at deconstructing some of the harmful traits and unhelpful behaviors that can keep a relationship from growing and thriving. Then in the part that follows we'll look at creating and building some healthy habits and highly effective practices into your marriage union.

As we've said in this chapter and as we'll keep on explaining in the pages ahead, successful marriages need more TV—a *lot* more. Learning to be transparent and vulnerable may be a difficult part of your personal journey, but it also may be the most rewarding.

TV will improve your friendships and personal relationships. People may like you because of your good qualities, but they'll *love* you for being honest, open, and revealing. It is this extra dimension that moves relationships to the next level—and the level beyond that. Within the context of marriage, TV takes you places you haven't been before, places you may not have believed would be possible for the two of you to achieve and explore.

But before we go further in unpacking the nature of TV and how to develop it, let's take a few pages to look at what happens when couples marry without TV.

part two:

de/construction

de/construction:
an ongoing process of
removing the barriers and obstacles
that may prevent understanding;
similar to "unbuild"
or take apart

2

Melting the Masks

*Behold, you delight in truth
in the inward being.*

—Psalm 51:6

What happens when we wear misleading masks while we are dating, courting, and even planning a new life together? What is the impact on a relationship if one person hides his or her true identity behind layers of carefully constructed falsehoods? Such deceptions can continue successfully for weeks, months, or even years before a sudden revelation shocks a hidden reality to the surface. In some cases the truth is revealed only after someone dies—only then does the mask drop away.

As this book is being written, a well-known minister has lost his public standing and his primary employment. He appears to have preached and proclaimed one set of values while secretly living out the very opposite of his public proclamation. Cynical observers may decry this as yet another example of hypocrisy in the pulpit. Yet such cases are in no way confined to people in public life or in ministry, or to persons of faith. Rather, these cases exemplify the dismal daily reality of many married persons who are suddenly surprised by a previously unknown and undisclosed element of their partner's existence.

An extremely horrible crime or the public disgrace of a prominent religious figure will be sure to make headlines. It may always be so in a scandal-driven and publicity-seeking news environment. Yet many ordinary adults suffer from exactly the same set of symptoms: a life partner who has, for whatever reason and with whatever intentions, deceived them about his or her true nature.

When we advocate more TV—more transparency and more vulnerability—this is the situation that propels us. All too often as family counselors we deal with the agonizing aftermath of deception, misdirection, and the wearing of misleading masks.

What is needed is the careful and attentive deconstruction of these masks, so that the actual nature and character of the person can be seen and known. Too often the masks are not deconstructed until dramatic revelations force the truth out into the public square. Only then, for the first time, do friends and family begin to comprehend the inner compulsions of someone they thought they knew.

There must be a better way to live, grow, and form relationships!

Up there at the front of the wedding chapel, a well-dressed couple stands together holding hands and saying vows. Promises are made, candles are lit, and music plays. At some point a minister makes a speech about the virtue of staying together for life. Friends applaud, families cheer, and everyone enjoys the reception.

Yet what if one member of the new couple—the bride or the groom—chooses to wear a mask that conceals difficult or discordant inner issues? What if one of the parties is getting married to an attractive stranger, a person deeply unknown to them?

The result is the opposite of intimacy. It's having the appearance of a relationship while in fact there is nothing of substance underneath. Despite the best intentions of clergy and counselors, sometimes persons do marry while wearing masks—and the implications resonate in today's divorce statistics and broken families.

Within the few brief pages of this chapter, we'll look at cases in which mask-wearing eventually ended in the destruction of a marriage and the meltdown and loss of family units, careers, and ministries. When one member of the couple insists on hiding away an inner life that is far different than their public one, the outcome will likely be tragic. And when the facts do come to light, the shock and trauma may permanently damage not only the relationship but also the inner life of both adults.

This is why, before taking deeper looks at transparency and intimacy, we need to take a careful and informed look at what happens when transparency does not exist, and when intimacy is feigned or implied without being truly realized. We need to understand what the risks are and where the dangers lie. For without this, we may perpetuate the pattern of uniting strangers in holy matrimony, realizing only later that there were topics we should have discussed, lines of questioning we should have pursued, and possible danger signs we should have noticed.

Failure to acknowledge reality does not change the facts. For this reason, we're about to take a look at what happens when someone marries another while wearing a misleading mask. We'll also see what happens in an existing marriage when one partner decides to embark upon a secret life, hiding away part of his or her existence behind a web of lies and deceit. Finally, we'll look at a new invader destroying the family, as couples discover the high price of unresolved sexual addictions and particularly the lure of Internet pornography.

The Great Pretender: How Rare?

Martin and Amy meet while attending a large church. Martin is a promising young seminary student with a bright future, and Amy has graduated from a small Christian college and is the assistant manager of a women's clothing store in a large suburban mall. The two begin dating. Their conversations are filled with laughter and sharp wit. They share the same quizzical, ironic sense of humor. Both of them enjoy finding the bizarre and unpredictable quirks in daily life.

Many of their friends tell them, "You two are perfect for each other!"

Although Amy has dated some, she has never had a serious relationship, certainly never one during which she contemplated marriage. It appears that Martin's background is very similar—a few dates along the way, but he's never been involved with anyone in a serious, lengthy, committed relationship. Gradually these two begin working their way toward togetherness. As they do so, both of their families are excited and running more than a little bit ahead of schedule.

"You should marry him," Amy's mother advises her one afternoon. "It's not like you're getting any younger! The good guys are rare, and you need to hang on to them when you find them." This is the first time Amy's mother has pushed her toward marrying a specific person. Their previous conversations have all been about getting married, but not to a here-and-now, present and dating person Amy actually knows and cares about.

Martin's mother behaves in much the same way. Excited and glad that her son is finally in a serious relationship, she expresses her feelings strongly. She is also insistent. "Amy seems like such a nice girl," Martin's mother frequently tells him. "What are you waiting for? Do you think the world is full of nice girls?"

These mothers are typical of many of today's parents. Faced with circumstances that appear favorable and a dating prospect whose public persona is acceptable, many moms and dads are delighted to give away their child in marriage. Driven by a desire for grandchildren or by noble motives of wanting their child's happiness, parents sometimes push their young adult offspring into marrying too quickly or without adequate preparation. Or, in many cases, into marrying the wrong type of person.

Amy remembers feeling pressured, but admits she was already going in the same direction, already thinking and dreaming about the possibility of someday marrying Martin. When he finally does propose to her, on a romantic evening with candles lit and a lovely hillside view, Amy is literally swept off her feet. She says an immediate and grateful yes. She can't wait to tell her parents; everyone shares her joy.

The new couple is married by Amy's minister without any pre-marriage counseling. They meet with him a few times before the ceremony, mostly to plan the wedding, but there is no discussion of communication issues, conflict resolution, managing money, or any of the topics marriage counseling generally covers.

Martin and Amy's large-church wedding is ornate and a bit too expensive—but after all, how often do you get married? Both families help out somewhat with the many expenses. Despite this assistance, the new couple—Martin is still in graduate school—faces a load of debt from the wedding and honeymoon as they begin their new life together.

Children happen. Two girls are born into their household within the next five years. Martin graduates seminary and gets an associate pastor position at a large church in another state, and the two move away from family and friends. Martin's charm and sense of humor serve him well—he is popular at their new church. To all appearances the young couple is happy, the children are healthy, and all is well.

Amy is lonely at times during these early years of marriage, but does not consider this to be abnormal or problematic. "Martin spent a lot of time studying," Amy recalls. "Especially that last year of seminary while I was pregnant with Beth—our first—he was gone a lot. He spent a lot of hours in the library at the seminary, doing research and writing papers. He wasn't home very much that year."

As they transition into Martin's first pastoral assignment, Amy is still lonely. She tells herself that many wives feel the same way. What about doctors' wives, the wives of police officers, the wives of military personnel serving in the Middle East and elsewhere? Amy tells herself that her own situation is neither better nor worse than many others. She makes an uneasy peace with her feelings of loneliness, believing them to be "a season" in the marriage that will surely change for the better in the days ahead.

Meanwhile, as he faces the demands of parish ministry, Martin is away from his family for many hours at a time. Amy often feels like a single parent, caring for two children and essentially raising them alone. It can be a demanding life, but she flexes with the challenges. She loves her husband, she loves her children; she believes that overall her marriage is no worse than most, probably better than many. She tries to have a positive attitude and keep hoping for the best.

Seven years into their marriage, Amy's world as the mother of two growing girls and the wife of a popular associate pastor falls apart when her husband is abruptly fired. Martin comes home and tells his wife he's been terminated, but does not offer any explanations or reasons. It's a nightmare scenario for Amy—how will she explain this situation to her parents, her family, and her friends?

This is totally unfair! Amy remembers thinking. She's ready to launch a campaign to save her husband's job. After all, Martin is popular in the congregation. Martin hasn't said or done anything that would cause him to merit being terminated.

Several weeks later, as the dust settles, Martin drops another bombshell. No matter how often she replays her mental tape of this conversation, Amy is still unable to process and accept its meaning. To her, it still doesn't seem real.

"I just think I'll be happier moving in with Mark," Martin confides to his wife. "I'm tired of pretending to be something I'm not. With Mark, I can be who I really am."

Did she hear him correctly? Has her husband of seven years just described his sudden love for—another man?

Words like *shocked* and *distraught* do not begin to describe Amy's reactions. As time passes she discovers that Martin lost his job because his ongoing affair with another man in the congregation became known to several other members of the pastoral staff. Confronted with news of the affair by the senior pastor, Martin not only admits to his gay lifestyle but also tells his employer he prefers the gay relationship to the heterosexual marriage he has "suffered through" for the past seven years.

The matter is dealt with privately. Most people in the congregation never learn the true nature of Martin's termination. From the pulpit a senior staff member informs the parish that "Martin has resigned his position in ministry." Although gossip and speculation are rampant for a time, no one suspects the truth—Martin is leaving his wife and pursuing an ongoing relationship with a person of the same sex.

This choice, to which Martin clings after numerous appeals from church leaders and others that he prayerfully reconsider, effectively ends Martin's career in pastoral ministry at this local church, and within its denomination as well. Confused and angry, Amy cannot even begin to process her feelings.

"Was my entire marriage a lie?" she asks herself and others. "Was any of it genuine and real? Was Martin always gay, and if so, why didn't I know it until now?"

No one answers her, and perhaps no one can.

Martin is gone, and Amy's previous life is shattered. What and how will she tell her children about their father's sudden absence from the home? What will be the nature of her relationship with Martin in the days ahead? She is bitter, angry, frustrated, depressed…and does not know where to turn.

A devoted husband, a caring father, a gifted seminary student, a talented young associate pastor—Martin appears to be all of these things. There is some truth to most of these appearances, yet none of them tells the complete story.

Martin does well in school; he makes very good grades and wins several awards among the members of his graduating class. He preaches effectively. His assigned times of preaching the sermon in chapel are well-attended and popular among the other students at the seminary. He is succeeding as he serves in his very first congregation. Many people respond positively to his messages and also to him personally. His senior pastor has high praise for his work in the pulpit and for his warm, winning ways with members of the congregation and community.

Martin demonstrates a reasonable level of care for his children. He brings home a regular paycheck, makes sure they have a roof over their heads and food for their table, and at times he interacts with them in a fatherly way, reading stories to them or playing games. He is not without love for his children, and his apparent care for them is genuine.

Martin seems to be a devoted husband. He does not flirt with the young women of the church, some of whom definitely flirt with him with varying intentions. He comes home to his wife, shares a marriage bed with her, and is involved with her in what Amy describes as a normal, healthy, active sex life. Family and friends would tell you that Martin is a good husband. His wife would concur: Martin may spend long hours doing ministry, but isn't that a holy choice? After all, he is serving a higher power.

> Looking back at two years, seven years, or twenty years of marriage, they ask the same kind of questions that haunt Amy after Martin leaves her. "Was it all a lie? Was *anything* real?"

However, there is also another factor at work in the equation of Martin's personhood. This x-factor is why Martin wears a mask. Deep inside he is drawn to sexual encounters with other males. This inner compulsion drives him to seek male friendships for sexual purposes, regardless of his marital status, family life, or role in ministry.

No one suspects this reality besides other males who share the same orientation and desires. These men find each other, within churches and outside of them. They tend to recognize their common ground, often without words being spoken. (Anecdotal surveys indicate that the percentage of those who pursue homosexual relationships within the churched population is essentially the same as among the general population.)

It turns out that Martin had sexual encounters with other males during his college years and also during his seminary training. Some of his sexual partners were other seminarians. During the time that Martin was dating Amy, getting closer to Amy, and proposing to Amy, he was also continuing to sexually interact with other men and actively seek gay companionship. By his own later confession, dating and marrying Amy did not interrupt his steady penchant for gay sex with numerous short-term partners.

This pattern continues as Martin becomes a father, graduates from seminary, and enters the professional ministry. He has lived this duplicity for a long time. Living a public life as a straight husband, caring father, and outgoing minister (wearing the mask) while also having a secret life (in which he acts out an entirely different role) has become a normative part of his existence.

Although the specific details of Martin's life are unique, the general outline is much less rare than you might expect. There are a lot of married women in North America who come home to empty houses, only to learn that their husbands have not only left them—they have left them for other men. These women are abandoned by masked men who have hidden their preferences behind the facade of typical, everyday married lives. Few of them were aware of their husbands' secret proclivities, and most of them are genuinely shocked and deeply traumatized by the revelation that their life partner seeks out or prefers homosexual relationships.

We have also dealt with men abandoned by their wives—wives who chose to leave their husbands in order to pursue relationships with women. Confused and often deeply hurting, these husbands struggle to process their previous experience as part of a seemingly healthy and normal marriage.

Looking back at two years, seven years, or twenty years of marriage, they ask the same kind of questions that haunt Amy after Martin leaves her.

"Was it all a lie? Was *anything* real?"

The Absentee Heart: When a Partner Wanders

In another state thousands of miles away, Gerald and Susan have been married for more than 12 years. They're active in their church, serving various ministry roles in music and worship (Susan) and in financial administration (Gerald).

Both of them are employed full-time outside their home. In the upscale suburban community in which they reside, it is almost impossible to sustain a mortgage with only one income. Although Gerald's job pays very well, his upper-middle-class income isn't high enough to keep the mortgage paid and the utilities turned on, plus take care of school clothing and frequent orthodonture for the kids. Susan works full-time because both she and Gerald regard it as economically necessary.

Their three young children are latchkey kids, coming home from school to an empty house. This is "normal" for them—it's the only life they have known from birth. Susan takes a few weeks off after each birth, then returns immediately to her job. The children are in day care during their early years, moving into pre-K programs as they reach the appropriate age, and then they transition to regular school. The community has a 12-month, year-round school schedule, which is popular with working parents.

Gerald and Susan mentor married couples in their church. They teach a video-based class about communication in marriage, which is offered on a recurring cycle. They have many friends in the congregation…although there is never enough time to really develop closeness and intimacy in these friendships because everyone is far too busy. Those who know them consider them a model married couple in many ways. They seem to have it all together and they appear to be very happy.

Interviewed later, family members and a few friends volunteer the fact that they never suspected anything was amiss in the couple's relationship. On the contrary, most outsiders admired Gerald and Susan's marriage and considered it exemplary.

Gerald enjoys being considered a "success" among his peers at church and within the community. His impressive home in a gated subdivision reflects his social standing. The family's late-model SUV is one of three vehicles the two of them own and is occasionally used to tow a ski boat to a nearby lake on summer weekends. As far as Gerald knows, everyone else wants to be him: He's living the American dream.

Then one day the dream shatters.

In a note penned and left at his bedside, Susan informs Gerald she is leaving him, she is "tired of pretending to love him," and she is moving in with her true love, a co-worker. As Gerald reads the note he gets short of breath, his heart skips a few beats, and he begins to sweat profusely. At first he thinks he's having a heart attack.

Not knowing what to tell his children, Gerald says nothing to them in the early days after finding Susan's note. After several traumatic weeks of gradually unfolding revelations, more of the truth begins to emerge. For nearly five years, Susan has been sexually involved with a married co-worker. "I really consider myself more married to him than I am to you," she informs her husband in a brief text message she sends to his cell phone. "There's no comparison between the two relationships. I am totally in love with him, not you."

Gerald attempts to process this information. For the past five years his wife has been a prominent member of the praise team at their church, leading choruses and songs about how much she loves God—then she's rushed out of the sanctuary to commit adultery, breaking one of His major commandments. She has conducted an ongoing affair with someone else who is also breaking God's laws, cheating on his spouse.

None of this makes sense. The more Gerald thinks about it, the less he is able to comprehend that his wife is actually being unfaithful to him, and that she has been unfaithful to him repeatedly and habitually over a long period of time. No matter how much he thinks about it or even prays about it, Gerald cannot get past the feeling that this is surreal, that it can't actually be happening…he will awaken one morning and discover it's all just a bad dream.

He reflects on the condition of his marriage recently. Susan has seemed to be a normal, apparently satisfied, reasonably well-adjusted wife during the entire duration of her extramarital affair. They have had what Gerald considers to be a normal sex life, perhaps not frequent enough but still fulfilling.

What went wrong? When and how did the marriage derail?

Gerald drops his church responsibilities, struggles with what and how much to tell his children, and begins a depressive cycle that will last nearly three years, during which he is the primary caregiver for his growing kids. His children are angry at God, angry at their mother, and often just angry in general. They act out in typical ways—their grades suffer and two of the three have discipline problems at school. Family life deteriorates and Gerald's depression intensifies.

Susan does not return to her husband and family. On the contrary she files for a divorce, seeking—among other things—the house she and Gerald have shared in the gated community. She does not seek primary custody of her children; all she wants is the right to visit them now and then, on her own schedule and on her own terms.

She has not only walked away from her marriage to Gerald, she has apparently abandoned being a mother also, turning her back on three children whose lives will never be the same. Susan chooses to move in with her lover and begin a whole new life for herself, as if her previous marriage and family did not exist.

Her now ex-husband, who suddenly feels he's lived a very sheltered life in a perplexing and unjust world, does not understand any of this. The few friends he confides in do not understand it either and cannot help him. Gerald withdraws from his previous patterns and enters a world of sleep-deprived single parenting, struggling to help his kids survive. He loses sleep, he gains weight, and he searches for answers that he cannot find.

He asks a lot of questions, but no one seems able to help him. He blames himself for his wife's departure, but can't identify what he did—or failed to do—that eroded the basis of the relationship and caused his wife to look for love elsewhere.

If he doesn't know what he did, how can he possibly change? Gerald internalizes a deep sense of failure, believing Susan's absence to be largely an indictment of his lack of attention, respect, or affection.

A happily married couple, active mentors for other marriages, picture-perfect parents of three growing young children—this is how things appear to those who look at Gerald and Susan from a distance.

Several new cars in the driveway, a fine "estate home" in a gated neighborhood—things must be going quite well in their financial lives as well as in their marriage.

A worship leader in the church, one with a ready smile and engaging personal charm, someone who makes others feel good just by being around her—this is another way that many people see and describe Susan. "She's the heart of the worship team," some church members believe and express.

"I love seeing her smile on Sunday," others add.

Each of these facets of Susan's life contains an element of truth. She and her husband are thriving in economic terms. Their children are cared for, although not by stay-at-home, readily accessible parents. The couple really does teach marriage lessons and communication techniques to other couples, and there is nothing invalid about this instruction or the value of it. There are elements of truth in all these appearances. These virtues are not invalidated simply because they form an incomplete picture.

Susan isn't pretending to be a wife—she *is* one. In public, especially at church, she smiles at her husband and fusses over her children, making sure their behavior is acceptable and their clothes are neat and clean. Other women watch her with envy and wish that they too had so much going for them. How wonderful it must be, to be Susan! Who wouldn't trade places with her, or at least trade houses? Susan has it all.

There is also another factor, however, in the equation of Susan's personhood. Just as with Martin, this x-factor lies behind the mask that Susan wears. Deep inside she is unhappy in her marriage, or perhaps bored, or maybe she is drawn to the possibility of a "forbidden" romance. Through all of this she keeps her mask firmly in place, not showing her husband, children, family, and friends any glimpse of her hidden nature and her divided desires.

A friendship begins. Then it extends past the godly, ethical boundaries for such friendships when both parties are married to others. This friendship becomes a fatal attraction. Sexual activity happens.

The sexual activity becomes a recurring pattern, and Susan finds herself bonding more deeply with her secret lover than with her public husband.

She goes forward with all of her normal activities. She has sexual relations with her husband; she cares for her children and makes sure their basic needs are met. She goes to church, strides up to the platform, and sings the praise choruses in a clear voice and with a ready smile. She worships God and she sways with the music.

Through all of this she is wearing a mask. She is keeping hidden a secret and growing part of her life that is threatening to break out and take over. Months fold into years and it becomes normative for Susan to wear the mask in her public roles, then sneak off to find illusory contentment in the bed of a man who is not her husband.

Again, as in Martin's case, the specific details of Susan's private life are unique. But the general outline is much more common than you might expect. There are a lot of married women and married men—including within our churches and sometimes among the leadership and staff—who wear masks of faithfulness to their partners, attentiveness to their children, and devotion to God. Yet behind these masks another truth rises up and insists on being acknowledged: These same married women and men are sexually involved outside of their marriages, perhaps with people who are also married. Emotionally and sexually, they are going places they may never have intended to go, but now they're firmly caught in a trap of their own making. Their secret lives are ready to boil over at any moment, scalding and scarring those who love them and depend on them—and probably others as well.

When the affair becomes public, pain explodes into the public arena and also within the heart of the abandoned husband or wife. Like Gerald, many of those who are abandoned carry layers of guilt, believing that somehow they are responsible for their partner's unwise behavior and destructive choices.

"I wish I had another chance to love her better," Gerald laments at one point. "Maybe I could have prevented this."

Reality suggests otherwise. Deceitful partners are responsible for their own choices and may not have been kept from straying regardless of how much love, respect, and affection existed in their marriage.

It's mostly my fault, Gerald tells himself often. *I drove her away.*

The reality, in Susan's case and many others, is that Susan did her own driving.

A Hidden Self: Addictions and Self-Destruction

Kirk and Shelley get remarried. Residents of the Atlantic seaboard, both have prior experience with marriage—she has been married twice before, he once previously. Financially challenged, they put together a small wedding attended by a few family members and some close friends. They begin a new life with a big dose of hope and anticipation, firmly believing that all will be well.

Kirk's children from his prior marriage are grown adults. None of them will live at home, although Kirk's youngest son, who attends a nearby college, will stop by and visit the family at times. Meanwhile Michelle's children are all in school; she has three girls from 9 to 14 years old. The three girls have two different biological fathers from Shelley's two previous marriages.

Kirk is a low-key, anything-goes father figure for the three girls. Shelley finds herself wishing that Kirk would be firmer, that he would back her up on her standards and rules, and that he would step up to the mark and become "the man of the house." Shelley's oldest daughter is loud and sometimes rebellious, arguing with her mother, slamming doors, and hiding in her room for long periods of time. Shelley wishes Kirk would make these behaviors stop—it's a man's job to rule the house, she fervently believes.

They attend a church of the same denomination in which Shelley was raised. The new family's church attendance is sporadic because Kirk loves to barbecue outdoors and then watch football on Sundays. This hinders or prevents church attendance, especially during the fall. They send the girls to children's events (the younger two) and to youth events (the oldest girl), but they rarely participate in church activities as a group.

Eighteen months into the new union Shelley is fairly satisfied. Kirk is less demanding sexually than her previous (second) husband; their physical union is close but not intense. Kirk has a good job and shares freely from his income, supporting the needs of the family. Kirk's grown children do not seem upset or offended by the new marriage. In fact, Kirk's only daughter actually reaches out to connect with Shelley and "welcome her to the family"—inviting her to coffee at Starbucks from time to time.

Shelley is more at ease and feels more secure than at any previous time in her life. She believes the relationship is basically solid, and all is well. Perhaps this third marriage will actually thrive and go the distance. Against all odds, maybe this is the union that will endure for a lifetime. Shelley is ready for that—more than ready.

One cold winter day her marriage hits the rocks in a most unexpected fashion.

Kirk has his personal computer set up in the den. Others in the family are not allowed to use it. Generous with his money, Kirk has purchased a family computer, which stays in the kitchen. The girls can check their e-mail, surf the Internet, and do their homework on the family computer, but they are not allowed to touch their stepdad's. That one is off limits to everyone, including Shelley. Kirk explains it's needed for work—it's a business computer and not intended for playing games.

Oldest daughter Melody, always testing the rules, decides to disobey and use Kirk's computer while he's not home. She chooses a perfect time, while Kirk is still at work and Shelley is picking up the other girls from school. Melody rides the bus every day and is normally the first one home, and she can hardly wait to sneak into the den and carry out her plan.

Alone in an empty house, Melody fires up the computer. There's no password in place. But instead of doing the usual sort of thing,

Melody decides she'll rummage around in Kirk's computer files, finding out what's he's got stored away on his hard drive. What does all this business stuff look like?

You have probably already guessed what she finds. Stashed away are hundreds of images of hard-core pornography, including some of the worst and most violent forms available. Melody, who has grown up watching MTV and who jokes with her friends in coarse and quite explicit ways, is nonetheless shocked by the ugly, outright evil nature of what she is seeing. She is also intrigued by it. She looks through dozens of hard-core photos, home alone and with no one to prevent her from doing so. She loses track of what time it is, taken captive by a whole new world of sensual imagery. Despite her intention to do so, she can't quite tear her eyes away from the screen.

Time passes. Melody is absorbed in her computer search.

Into the den march Shelley and the other two girls. Shelley, immediately seeing that Melody is breaking the rules, begins yelling. "Get away from that terminal right now!" she shouts from across the room, not yet fully grasping the situation. "That's Kirk's computer, and you know you're not allowed to use it! Stop it and go to your room!"

Melody flashes her mother a sly grin. "Mom," she says sweetly, "why don't you come over here and look at what Kirk has on his computer?"

Mom does.

Shelley's background and experience are more sheltered than that of her own 14-year-old daughter, and at first she's too shocked to speak. She stares at the computer screen in stunned silence, not able to accept or grasp what she is seeing.

"There are hundreds of these, Mom," Melody tells her mother. "Some are even worse than this one!"

Shelley recovers her composure when she realizes her two younger daughters are on their way across the room, eager to see what all the discussion is about. "Turn that thing off!" she yells at Melody. "Turn it off quick!"

By the time Kirk gets home from work, his remarriage is essentially history. Shelley has already decided she won't expose her impressionable young girls to a father figure who stashes hard-core, violent pornography on his personal computer, for purposes she can only guess at. There's nothing to discuss, as she sees it.

"I'm leaving you," she tells Kirk when he walks in the door. Seeing the dumbfounded look on his face, she explains to him exactly why she is gone for good.

An apparently successful remarriage, a happy couple, and three young girls who have gained a kind and caring stepfather. Kirk is generous with his money, stable, and solidly employed. He provides for his new family's financial needs and, in his own way, cares for their emotional needs also. Shelley considers him a loving husband.

By all appearances this blended family is poised to beat the odds. There aren't the usual arguments over how to raise the children or how to spend the money. Although there are ex-spouses to deal with, none of these pose an active risk to the new union. Even the children from previous marriages seem to be adjusting to Kirk and Shelley's decision to marry. The couple appears to have an above-average chance of going the distance and living out a lasting union.

There is a measure of truth in all of these appearances, yet there is another factor at work in the equation of Kirk's life. This x-factor is hidden by the mask Kirk wears with his wife and around his step-kids. Behind the mask Kirk is addicted to Internet pornography—an addiction shared by millions of men in North America, including men who are in roles of ministry and service. (Although proportionately a much smaller number, some women are apparently addicted as well, according to contemporary surveys.)

On the surface Kirk is a caring father, a responsible provider, a stable person. Judging by outward appearances and public evidence, the family does not seem to have unusual or highly significant challenges to address. Yet Kirk has a secret life behind the mask he wears, a life waiting to break into the open and destroy his new family. He lives for his next fix of Internet porn—preferring the glow of his computer screen to the company of his attractive real-life marriage partner. Although he believes he is fully in control of his behavior, he resembles many others with all types of addiction. They underestimate and ignore the depth of their involvement and the degree to which they are hooked by drugs, alcohol, or pornography.

For Shelley, the decision is simple: a no-brainer. "Kirk is a really nice guy," she says later. "I honestly hope he gets some help. But while he's getting that help, me and my girls are going to stay a long way away from him. This marriage is over—and I'm not going back to him as long as I have kids."

Shelley's decision may not reflect the way all wives react when they find out that their husbands have secret sexual addictions. Yet Shelley is not alone in deciding to abandon such a husband rather than raise children in an environment that seems tainted by images of degrading, dehumanizing sexual behavior. Sexual addictions are responsible for the end of many marriages and remarriages; Shelley's choice is the same one that many others, in similar situations, have made.

Owning Up to the Mask: Exploring the Disconnect

A male seminary student who becomes a young married pastor while pursuing sexual relationships with other men. A married woman who mentors and teaches others about marriage and family values, smiles and leads public worship in a thriving church, then drives out of the parking lot and carries on a multiyear affair with a man who is married to someone else. A caring stepfather who guards the safety and well-being of four women in his newly blended family, yet at the same time secretly views and collects images of violent, degrading acts against anonymous women.

The common element in each of these stories is the presence of a severe disconnect between the outward appearance of a person— including a public life that may exhibit commendable or virtuous behavior—and a reality concealed behind the public mask that conflicts with and contradicts the visible evidence. It's a theme that is well explored in literature and entertainment, *Dr. Jekyll and Mr. Hyde* being a prime example. Similar stories and legends tell of characters who are acceptable by day and then are transformed into werewolves or vampires at night, wreaking havoc in villages or terrorizing the countryside. These morality tales may simply be telling us that there is a potential for good and evil inside every human, and that these two forces play out in different ways in every life.

Scripture brings us another perspective here. "Man looks on the outward appearance, but the Lord looks on the heart" (1 Samuel 16:7). In other words, we humans see only the visible evidence on the surface: the public masks. Yet when God looks at a human life, He sees with divine eyes, penetrating the masks and looking directly at the moral and spiritual reality underneath. People are often deceived by the outward appearance of a person; God always sees the truth behind the mask.

As we apply these thoughts to the topic of dating and relationships, two immediate challenges demand attention. First, the person we are befriending or dating or courting may have inner desires or secret behaviors that are in conflict with the public evidence we see. This possibility should demand our full attention—not in a jaded, cynical way, but in a sincere effort to get to know someone as deeply as possible before making a lifelong commitment.

Second, the question becomes one to pose to the person in the mirror. To what extent in my own life am I acting one way in public (wearing a mask) while concealing a habit or tendency or nature that takes me in a completely different direction? In the words of the powerful old spiritual, "Not my brother, not my sister, but it's me, O Lord—standin' in the need of prayer." Most of us, especially in the rituals of romance, make a very determined effort to look our best, sound our best, and do our best. We disguise our actual tendencies and typical behaviors by putting on a mask. We don't think of this as being deceptive; we justify this as "putting our best foot forward" or as "being our best selves." Such efforts usually succeed—temporarily. Yet all the while there is a time bomb ticking away in the background, waiting to detonate.

Both of these issues need our fearless exploration. Am I marrying someone with a hidden life or unseen tendencies? I need to know *now*, not find out later. And within my own heart and life, am I concealing destructive behaviors or patterns that should be disclosed, admitted, and worked through *now*—before I join in marriage?

For ministers, marriage counselors, and others, the challenge is to help people explore these questions *before* the wedding ceremony, rather than being surprised later. Although difficult, these are exactly the kinds of questions that need to be raised while there is still time for an engaged adult to say "no" or "later"...rather than rushing ahead and pledging his or her life to a mask-wearing partner.

Melting the Masks: Models that Actually Work

Effective, proven, mask-melting counseling resources are available from a variety of sources. The Celebrate Recovery (CR) movement, among many other helpful developments in modern community life, helps adults break the power of secret addictions and move forward toward healthy, functional lives and successful marriages and families.

One of the reasons the Celebrate Recovery program is growing so rapidly is that so many adults struggle with issues exactly like we are discussing in this chapter. Within a CR small group, it is possible to admit, discuss, and repent of unhealthy habits and practices while finding the grace to build a new life. Birthed on the West Coast, the Celebrate Recovery movement is expanding in all directions, perhaps because it is founded on the premise that personal honesty is the best way forward for all of us.

Buddy Davis, who directs a busy and successful Celebrate Recovery program in the metro Tulsa area, calls working with CR "a front-row seat for watching changed lives—including my own." Davis, together with his wife, Alicia, is pioneering new frontiers in CR as he integrates Oklahoma state prisoners and their families into recovery groups. His work has won him wide respect in Tulsa and beyond.

Among others, divorced adults often find themselves drawn to CR groups because they are places where it is entirely safe to admit and process anger, admit and recover from sexual addiction, or gain victory over addiction to painkillers or alcohol and other destructive habits. By working through a 12-step program similar to that pioneered by Alcoholics Anonymous, those in Celebrate Recovery begin to drop their masks, admit their weaknesses, and move toward healthy patterns of living.

For example, in step 4 of the 12 steps, adults involved in CR make a "searching and fearless moral inventory" as they seek to face and admit the deep struggles of their inner selves. This is the time when many people begin to make meaningful progress toward maturity, finally putting away the patterns and habits of childhood and adolescence. Surrounded by others with whom they are vulnerable and to whom they are accountable, those involved in CR learn the blessing of intentional transparency. They also become skilled at seeing through the surface lies of those around them, thus helping other group members learn new patterns of honesty, openness, and self-disclosure. While finding help for themselves, CR group members invariably offer much help to others along the way.

Whether the secret struggle is sexual addiction, alcoholism, codependency, or one of many other issues, the Celebrate Recovery movement is designed to be a place where masks melt and adults interact with one another in accountable fellowship. Friendships formed in CR are rooted in reality, not public appearances. There's no room for pretense or pride when a small group of adults sits around a room openly confessing their struggles to one another and praying for each other.

Simply stated, there's a whole lot of TV in Celebrate Recovery, which is one reason we highly recommend it and, as often as possible, participate.

Courtship and Marriage: Too Often, the Masks Are Still in Place

Many marriages begin while the courtship phase is still in the "masks not yet slipped" stage of development. This deception may be relatively benign—she pretends to be a tidy and neat person yet in reality she is sloppy and disorganized. Or the disconnect may be deeper: He pretends to be heterosexual and faithful, while beneath the surface he gravitates to homosexual relationships, secretly living out the opposite of monogamy, as in the case of Martin and Amy.

Many of us wear masks of one kind or another, benign or otherwise. The presence of these masks is a powerful and compelling argument for making only slow, carefully counseled decisions about getting married or remarried. The more we hurry, the greater the possibility there will be surprises waiting for us later. Not many of these surprises will turn out to be happy and pleasant ones.

In the North America of the emerging twenty-first century, a lot of attention is being focused on helping couples be better prepared for marriage. Just as with many marriage resources the focus is on helping prospective couples learn how to communicate better, develop useful skills for resolving conflict in peaceful ways, and move toward unity in their approaches to financial management or the discipline of children.

All of these activities are useful and welcome. The skills being taught should help us form more lasting unions. We should welcome and encourage these helpful programs and practices. Yet such activities, useful as they are, do not engage the core problem we have been discussing, the problem that will undermine so many relationships at a later stage. This issue is that, to some extent, both parties in a relationship are wearing masks.

Marriages may survive this mutual mask-wearing for many seasons. Children are raised, careers arc upward, economic progress is made, and the marriage endures. Eventually comes retirement and old age—and the couple is still together. We regard these marriages as successful simply because they still exist. There has been no divorce. Yet within the walls of these marriages, behind closed doors where we are not invited, the relationship between the two married adults may be merely cordial or attentive, nothing more than pleasant or cooperative. Perhaps there may be a mutually agreeable level of tension that is accepted by both as normative and livable: "Aren't all marriages like this?"

What's Missing at the Core

What is missing in these apparently successful marriages is the core value we are exploring together in the pages of this book: intimacy. That is the stunning truth about many long-term marriages, including marriages between practicing Christians. These unions are places of physical intimacy (naked and unashamed), but in the deeper terms of personal identity, one or both parties keep their masks on forever, never risking the dangerous prospect of becoming fully known. These enduring marriages do not achieve interpersonal intimacy (emotional and spiritual) and may not even attempt it.

As Danielle asked in our opening chapter, *Is this all there is?* We hope, we long, we wish for something deeper—but if it's out there, we don't know where to look. Or perhaps we do know, somewhere inside our souls, but we are afraid to take the risk. Meanwhile we may live lives of quiet desperation, not quite believing that intimacy and closeness are possible for us, even if the lucky few do seem to find it.

The Journey to Intimacy

The pathway to spiritual and emotional intimacy is lit by torches of transparency. Transparency—being seen as we truly are—is the opposite of wearing masks. Instead of carefully crafting an outward appearance we deliberately strip away all of our masks, allowing our lover to know us at the fullest and deepest level. In the consuming fire of a close and meaningful relationship we allow our masks to melt away, burning up as chaff. For perhaps the first time in our lives, we enter a relationship as who we actually are.

The pathway to spiritual and emotional intimacy is marked by signposts of open vulnerability, times and places where we lower our guard and share the deepest parts of our hearts and souls with the partner to whom we've pledged ourselves for a lifetime. We strip off the emotional armor we wear in other settings, allowing our inner thoughts and ideas, our underlying values and desires, to be explored and known by the one who loves us.

There is so much risk in this—so much potential for rejection or abandonment or loss—that few of us will dare to be so vulnerable. Few attempt to achieve such transparency. Instead we hold ourselves back from the warming flames. We withdraw. We allow our marriage partner to believe a few little illusions about us, or perhaps we let them cling to a great number of major misconceptions—the same ones we have carefully created for the public in order to be accepted, respected, or valued by others. Our partners, who ought to know us better than anyone, are instead deceived.

We cultivate an image and we maintain it carefully. We choose a faux-union that keeps up appearances instead of daring the fiery, mask-melting gauntlet that burns our illusions to smoke, welding us together intimately.

If we deceive others we raise the probability that one day, perhaps soon, our inner life will explode into the open, causing pain and damage in all directions.

We can avoid this pain. But doing so requires the difficult work now, before we marry and before we form families. Or if we are already married, we can avoid this pain by finding a safe place to seek counsel, perhaps join a Celebrate Recovery group, and begin moving forward toward a life free from deception.

We need more TV. We need to form relationships based on who we actually are: works in process, incomplete persons, strong in some areas and very weak in others. Every one of us is on a journey…it's time to quit pretending otherwise.

Fear of being deeply and truly known
is a shelter for our wrongful pride.
We do not need such shelter.
We need a bonfire for our vanities.

3

Crumbling the Walls

The real voyage of discovery
consists not in seeking new landscapes...
but in seeing with new eyes.

—MARCEL PROUST

One of our casual friends, married for many years, was past middle age and nearing his retirement. David worked with this gentleman, who was a pleasant and agreeable co-worker. Although quiet and soft-spoken he had a sharp and hilarious wit—his quick sense of humor often surprised group meetings and frequently infused office dinner parties with zings of laughter. This man was fun to know and a great joy to work with. He was also quite good at his job in a printing-related industry.

Nearing age 60, he definitely smoked and drank too much. These things might eventually have caused or contributed to his death. As it was, however, he was sitting at home one night reading the newspaper after a long day's work when his wife apparently sneaked up behind, hit him over the head with a hammer, and killed him.

She later confessed to the crime; the case had a brief and sensationalized run in the local newspapers. Many of us from the office attended the somber funeral service. It was a sad and surreal ceremony, a bizarre twist at the end of a life lived—so far as any of us could tell—as a peaceful, agreeable citizen. Who knew that reading the sports pages in a comfortable chair at home could be deadly?

Though certainly more splashy and definitely more lethal than most marriages, our friend's dysfunctional and deadly relationship illustrates the fact that sometimes both parties within a marriage construct walls and barriers around themselves. They shut off their deep innermost feelings and remain separate and isolated, even from their life partner.

Such couples may functionally live in the same house as though they were single adults, not meaningfully or intensely connected with the person who daily shares their bathroom, kitchen, and living space. Over time, a life meant to be lived in unity becomes a walled-off existence of separate individuals. This kind of life can prove dangerous to the health of a marriage and apparently also to the health of a person who resides in such a marriage. When a marriage contains walls that divide the two partners into separate spheres of existence, trouble is often near.

Same Address, Separate Lives

Sometimes these walls of separation are more than a figure of speech. The 1993 movie *Dave,* which some suggest was modeled after an actual presidential marriage, depicts a U.S. president and wife who live together in the White House—officially—while each maintaining separate bedrooms and living separate lives. An icy chill permeates the relationship of these political veterans; they come together only when necessary, such as when campaigning for another office or when attending highly public events.

With the television cameras rolling and the press in attendance, the savvy but separate married adults present the image of a happily married couple, appearing to share the journey of life in harmony. They smile and interact with each other in a carefully scripted way that gives the appearance of romance, enduring companionship, and committed love.

Behind the closed doors of the White House, the walls between the two partners are not only emotional and relational, they are also structural: separate bedrooms with separate doors, each one at opposite ends of a lengthy hallway. White House staffers know the truth, but the public sees only the bright illusion.

It is often reported that many Hollywood marriages function in the same way. Two stars come together in a highly publicized romance, make a decision to marry, build or buy a fabulous house somewhere…but soon begin to live entirely separate lives. Eventually, in many cases, there is a legal and perhaps loudly acrimonious separation and divorce, yet long before the official termination of the marriage contract there are two separate persons, walled off from each other relationally and emotionally. They take separate vacations, travel in different groups, have different networks of friends, and move in entirely separate social circles.

We know of a couple with a highly public marriage ministry, and through contact with family and friends we're aware that behind the scenes, all is not well. On camera and in print, this couple exudes a highly radiant blazing-white-teeth-smiling cheerfulness about married life. Behind the scenes they fight, exhibit passive–aggressive tendencies, and are seldom directly involved in the discipline and raising of their own children.

Such segmented relationships are not confined to politics and entertainment. We all know from experience that many couples maintain the formal and legal existence of their marriage union while avoiding any semblance of closeness, intimacy, or togetherness. Some of them, for whatever reason, maintain the fiction among family and friends that they are "happily married," and since others neither reside with them nor have access to their private moments, this fiction can stay in place for long periods or even forever. Only the two partners know they live a life of isolation and withdrawal behind the pretense of a unified and healthy marriage…though other members of the household, especially adolescents and teens, may also know the secret behind their parents' cohabiting but separate lives.

The pews of churches are filled with couples like this, men and women who remain in sexual fidelity to their partners yet live as functional strangers. Friends and family see only the appearance of a successful, long-term marriage. There is no reason for co-workers or others to suspect otherwise because the partners do not fight in public and neither of them gossip about the other. The fiction remains intact and viable.

Yet what loneliness, despair, and cynicism fills these created-for-intimacy partners, residing in close proximity to each other and yet emotionally miles apart? Their children, who may reach teenage years before beginning to learn the truth, often decide not to marry as they reach adulthood. Jaded by coming of age in a home without married love, they decide that marriage itself is a sham, a meaningless custom that deserves to die away.

How should we view such loveless unions? Should we wish for these couples to divorce, so the inner reality becomes outwardly visible? God forbid. What we should hope, pray, and work toward is that one, preferably both, of the partners begins to actively crumble the walls that separate them, humbly and sincerely offering to conform the marriage to God's original blueprints. Having worked with troubled marriages for more than two decades, we have seen this happen. We have seen the walls start to crumble and a meaningful union begin to bloom in what once was a desert of separate lives.

For a marriage counselor this scenario is the equivalent of standing on the porch and watching the prodigal son return from a season of debauchery, wastefulness, and loss. There is an overwhelming joy in watching a couple begin to find fulfillment and intimacy, even when this occurs late in life and after several decades of an empty, unhealthy marriage relationship. The return of married love—or in some cases the firstfruits of married love after a long and loveless union—brings intense joy to the counselor, minister, grown children, or other friends and family who witness the miracle.

Only God makes love, and He can create it in the most unlikely places.

Crumbling the Walls: The Power of Surprising New Patterns

Connie and Bob are an illustration of crumbling the walls later in life. They were raised in the Midwest, they married at an early age, and the trajectory of their marriage relationship largely echoed their family histories. Both had parents who lived within an intact marriage, yet without exhibiting much joy and without expressing much affection—between themselves, to their children, or in outside circles such as relatives and friends.

Psychologists might consider the adults in such relationships to be repressed. Regardless of the diagnosis, there are tangible differences among cultures and among families regarding the way in which affection is expressed, how much affection is shown, and in what settings it is appropriate and customary to display affection. Some cultures, for instance, tend toward the stoic with regard to affection, emotions, and feelings. And in a very real sense each individual family creates and lives out its own culture, regardless of its ethnic origins or its socioeconomic status. Each family unit is a subculture within itself, having its own mores and values, its own styles and practices.

Some families are huggy havens, and some are definitely not. Some families kiss each other hello or goodbye, as many Europeans do upon greeting their friends. Other families do not display affection in a physical way, although the bonds of underlying warmth are strong and true. Cultural variables are always in place. One aspect of effective marriage counseling involves unpacking family histories and family cultures with regard to this exact variable: the expression of affection.

Bob and Connie each grew up observing and learning from parents who did not display affection. There were occasional moments of verbal praise for the kids, yet even these gifts were few and far between—lest the growing child somehow swell up with pride and become conceited (the work of the devil). Such cultural norms are not uncommon in the Midwest, particularly among those whose ancestors came from northern Europe.

This more repressed style of family interaction often holds true in families attending church in the upper Midwest. Affection exists but is not displayed in public, perhaps not even in the privacy of one's home. Among other social observers, Garrison Keillor brings upper Midwesterners and their stoic, reserved families to life with uncanny accuracy in his astute writings or hilarious radio programs. He is obviously drawing upon source material that is deeply rooted in the soil of his own upbringing.

Without consciously intending it, both Bob and Connie came to their marriage with this particular perception of the relationship between husband and wife. They did not show each other much physical affection, and they held back from displays of outward, visible warmth. They created or allowed emotional walls, without realizing that these patterns formed barriers that divided them as a couple.

Neither perceived this as a stumbling block or a problem within their marriage until their oldest daughter married a warm and outgoing young man from the Northwest. Watching the young couple date, become serious about each other, and eventually get married, Connie often found herself jealous. *It must be so wonderful,* Connie thought to herself as she watched her daughter and son-in-law embark on their married lives, *to share a union that is so close, so romantic, and so obviously fulfilling.*

Over time, Connie saw her own marriage with new eyes, believing that, in her own words, "more must be possible." But how could she and Bob get there? They had lived together for nearly 30 years by the time of these revelations, and both had long since adjusted to the way things were. They didn't dislike each other—there was actually a subterranean undercurrent of genuine love. It just didn't find its expression in outward, visible, newlywed-romantic types of ways.

Past 50, Connie suddenly wanted a lot more loving and a lot fewer walls.

As a religious woman, Connie didn't dream or scheme about running away with someone who was physically affectionate. Instead, she began to see her middle-aged, bulkier-over-time husband as someone with whom she could and would choose to display open affection.

She decided not to tell Bob what she was up to. Bob noticed anyway.

She began surprising her husband with long hugs, sweet compliments, and lengthy kisses at unexpected times. This was a radical departure from her previous patterns. Connie was learning a whole new way of relating to her husband and life partner. She was exploring previously uncharted territory and finding new ways to communicate.

To hear Connie tell the story, Bob initially shrank away from these overtures and seemed uncomfortable. At other times he would misread her signals, interpreting her sudden hugs as a desire for sex.

"It took me quite a while to break through his natural defenses," Connie laughs unself-consciously. "He put up with a lot from me in those days. He had no idea what was going on or why, but he was a pretty good sport about it most of the time."

Visitors to Bob and Connie's home today get a much different picture of the married relationship. Where previously there would have been physical distance between this husband and wife, now they frequently enter or leave a room together. Connie sometimes sits on Bob's lap or sits down very close to him and leans over onto his shoulder, relaxing. Both of them give and receive hugs, and both of them sometimes even allow their kisses to be seen by others—although not in public, not outside the home.

The crumbling of the behavioral walls between Connie and Bob has produced, according to each of them, a greater closeness emotionally. Neither one expected this; each regarded their marriage as "just fine" before the changes. Yet today they each report they feel closer. They feel more united as a couple and seem to be "more in love" than they were 10 or 20 years previous. Their new emotional closeness has been a direct consequence of learning a new style of relating to each other physically.

If Bob and Connie's parents could see the couple today, they'd be shocked. After their initial surprise wore off—and especially if they could watch the couple interact with each other over a period of time—these taciturn, repressed parents would probably be glad. Maybe even allow a tiny smile to curve up their lips, however briefly.

Sometimes, although perhaps not in public, even Mona Lisa smiles.

Sex and Intimacy: Very Separate Issues

It is completely possible for married couples to be sexually active with each other and yet remain emotionally distant from one another, separated behind conscious or unconscious walls. We discussed this earlier in our brief look at singles and sexuality—we spoke of these persons as "sexually active porcupines." Such behavior is not only possible, it may be normative for some.

A husband may complete the act of sex because his drive is still strong, because he wants to prove himself as a man, or simply because he enjoys the physical satisfaction. But he remains fully enclosed behind his emotional walls, keeping his thoughts and his feelings separate from the process of physical union.

A wife, particularly a Christian wife, may "go along with" her husband's sexual overtures, allowing the sexual process to come to its completion, yet without opening up to her feelings and emotions during the exchange. She may be angry at her husband yet still have sex. She may resent him and still dutifully "serve his needs" in the bedroom. She fulfills her sexual duties but does so in an aloof and detached way, not allowing herself to be present in the moment, actively enjoying the sexual dimensions of intimacy.

We will discuss sexuality more deeply in our next chapter, yet for this moment it needs to be observed that the act of sex can be shared—even repeatedly or frequently—between two persons who remain strangers to each other. This holds true whether they are sexually active singles or have been married to each other for many years or many decades.

Even among the married, physical walls lapse at times while emotional barriers stay firmly in place, unmoved and unchanging. This is why writers have called the sexual act "the little death"—on completion, it can bring a bittersweet loneliness and a sense of loss or absence that is tangible and surprising. Though couples unite in the closest form of physical embrace, yet they realize as they do so that even in sexual union, they are more distant and remote from one another than ever before.

Wired Differently: Comparing Intimacy for Men and Intimacy for Women

Much has been written about the differences between the sexes, with particular attention paid to the varying ways in which men and women think, feel, and express themselves emotionally. Books on these topics tend to sell very well, and seminars on these themes are well-attended. Celebrating and highlighting the differences between men and women appears to be popular in today's culture.

Bestselling author John Gray informs us that "men are from Mars." Gray gives women a planet of their own also; they get Venus. The primary content of Gray's books simply reveals to us that men and women think differently and act differently, particularly with regard to expressing their emotions and feelings. Gray then trains us to recognize our varying patterns of processing emotions and to be more receptive and understanding with our opposite-sex life partners.

In a very similar way, authors Bill and Pam Farrel coin the phrase "Men are like waffles." Skipping past other breakfast foods, the Farrels move to the dinner course and explain to us that "women are like spaghetti." This interesting blend of Italian and Scandinavian cooking makes for a good read. By all means pick up their book—what you'll discover is a lengthy and at times witty discussion of the fact that men and women think and act differently, especially with regard to how they explore and express their emotions and feelings. The Farrels unpack their picnic basket by telling us that men compartmentalize their lives (like the squares on waffles), while with women, one part of their lives spills into and connects with all the other parts of their lives (like strands of spaghetti on a plate).

Flush with creative genius, we've wanted to mimic these concepts with a book of our own. We are sad to report that *Men Are Like Dodges, Women Are Like Bentleys* has not yet been test-driven into a store near you. Perhaps shrewd veterans of the publishing industry are on their way to talk with us, but are delayed in heavy traffic. For now, go ahead and buy the books from John Gray and the Farrels. Maybe you'll be able to buy our highly original new Dodge/Bentley book a little farther down the road.

Separation Grows When We Don't Deal with It

The emotional walls between a husband and wife tend to get thicker and higher, stronger and more fortified as time passes. While there is no merit in assigning blame, it is often one partner who begins constructing the emotional walls first. Then the other partner responds by withdrawing emotionally or by building walls of his or her own. The more time that passes, the more normative it becomes for each spouse to exist in a walled-off world of isolation.

A woman, for example, has her feelings hurt by something her husband does or says, or perhaps by something he fails to say or do. She is offended by this or angry about it. How can her husband profess to love her while so obviously ignoring or attacking her? She nurses her disappointment or anger, hiding it away in her heart until it grows up into bitterness, resentment, or open antipathy and fighting. Once her mind-set is firmly established, future words and actions by her husband only confirm her suspicions: *He is uncaring, he is insensitive, he is too selfish, he doesn't love me.*

When we hold on to negative emotions they began to infect us at all levels of our consciousness. They change our outlook and mind-set, causing us to hear differently, think differently, feel differently, and act differently. There are many bitter, still-married wives whose descent into toxic resentment began when they chose to hold on to a few small slights or oversights in their husbands' words or behavior. Over time these small events solidified together, gathered new evidence around them, and formed a large and growing barrier between the woman and her husband.

When a woman walls herself off emotionally from her husband, holding on to her hurt feelings and her many grievances, the outcome is predictable. The marriage she believes to be weak actually weakens as a direct consequence of her own choice to become emotionally distant. Her husband, without understanding the process or knowing the extent of his previous wrongdoing, begins to lose interest in her as a person and build his own walls of privacy and personal space. He retreats into whatever form of satisfaction appeals to him. He may functionally abandon the marriage without ever leaving home or finding a new partner.

On the flip side, a man may have his feelings hurt because his wife rejects his physical and sexual advances, doesn't show much genuine interest in his hobbies or pursuits, or won't listen to his lengthy and involved stories about complex situations at work. His conclusions: She doesn't care about me, she isn't interested in my life, she doesn't love me anymore, she's frigid.

Over time these unfounded opinions harden into a deepening contempt for his wife and bring an openness and availability to other women who do love sports, who work near his cubicle or office, or who enjoy the same types of hobbies or conversations he does. Even a sexually faithful married husband may find himself paying lots of attention to a woman who is not his wife simply because she follows the Lakers, has always dreamed of attending a Final Four, or works at his company and thus understands and cares about its many challenges. While some of these dangerous relationships do eventually develop into sexual affairs, even the relationships that remain physically chaste may involve a degree of closeness and identification that is best reserved for our committed life partners.

When a husband allows his negative feelings about his wife to fester and the poison to work in deeper, he walls himself off from her, believing she doesn't care about him anymore. He may preserve the outward appearance of the marriage; he may never choose to have a sexual affair; yet he displays much more interest in women who are not his wife, giving them frequent bursts of positive attention and spending as much time around them as he possibly can. The result, obviously, is that the marriage union which he believes to be weak actually does weaken—a direct outcome of his own neglect and his choice to be emotionally isolated from the woman to whom he once pledged his permanent devotion and attentive care. As he continues to believe that his marriage is not fulfilling, he withdraws from it more and more. As a result, the state of his marriage often confirms his conclusions...largely because of his own behavior and choices.

These destructive patterns weaken whatever love remains in the marriage relationship and may presage a lonely husband's eventual involvement in sexual affairs, addiction to pornography, or other ways of detouring around intimacy with a life partner.

The Walls Must Come Down

Regardless of who constructs the walls or who begins building them first, the pathway to genuine intimacy is strewn with rubble: broken bits of brick and stone that fall away as the walls crumble and the couple finds or returns to a meaningful unity. No matter how the walls got there in the first place, it is a world of joy to watch them begin to crumble away. If you care about intimacy in a marriage, it's time your knuckles were bleeding: get out there and start tearing down the walls stone by stone.

Trapped in passive-aggressive patterns, many wives are unable or unwilling to tell their husbands how they're feeling or what they wish for within the context of a marriage. Convinced that their wives are frigid or distant, many husbands channel their emotional and perhaps their sexual energy in other directions. In either of these cases, the distressed adult is avoiding a problem and fleeing from it, rather than confronting the issues in a candid, direct, and useful manner.

The good news is that such patterns, no matter how firmly

entrenched and no matter how long they have existed, can be deliberately reversed. Couples with harmful or negative ways of relating to one another can and do learn healthier habits and practices. Through wise counseling, through programs such as PREP,* couples can learn the contours of healthy relationships and can immediately begin to improve the quality of their communication with each other.

Your Partner Is Not a Mind-Reader!

Ben and Sarah married after the briefest of courtships. By this we do not mean today's understanding of courtship as a structured alternative to dating. Rather, they met through mutual friends, rushed through a few weeks of passionate dating, and decided to get married. Both were nearing 30, and each for personal reasons was simply "ready" to get married and leave the single life behind.

Sarah came to the marriage with definite assumptions about the differing roles of the husband and the wife. While these expectations covered a broad spectrum of duties and functions, one of Sarah's principal expectations was that her husband would be the spiritual leader in their home. This, Sarah believed, was the biblical model for and description of marriage: Men lead in spiritual matters.

Although there were disappointments in other areas also, almost immediately Sarah began to despair of Ben's apparent lack of interest in spiritual growth. He went to church with her—she more or less insisted he do so—but except within the walls of the church, Sarah did not observe Ben praying, reading the Bible, seeking a relationship with God, or doing anything remotely spiritual. Sarah did learn that Ben had a passion for stock-car racing and the entire NASCAR

---

* Some states, such as Oklahoma, have begun offering PREP and other useful courses without charge to married couples. The Oklahoma Marriage Initiative goes even further: couples can attend useful courses for free, and can also receive a stipend to cover the cost of child care while the couple participates in a weekend retreat. With the financial obstacles removed, a couple literally has "no excuse" for not moving forward toward healthier and more constructive ways of relating to each other.

Oklahoma's experience is beginning to yield fruit: couples previously headed for divorce have turned around, rediscovered their attraction for each other, and begun the difficult work of dropping their masks, telling each other the truth, and working to build a lasting, healthy, and fulfilling marriage.

circuit. He could talk for hours about a certain driver, car, collision, or upcoming race. He would plunge into these discussions with obvious excitement and enthusiasm. Where was his passion, Sarah wondered, when it came to spiritual matters? Why couldn't Ben's walk with God inspire and animate him?

Once Sarah realized Ben lacked interest in learning more about spiritual things, she began to conclude that Ben was failing her as a husband. She went through the motions of being a wife, but on a daily basis she spent time feeling sorry for herself, wishing she had taken more time to choose a husband, dreaming about having a "godly" husband who would speak about the Bible or spiritual topics with the same passionate intensity Ben showed for "stupid cars."

Sarah began building an emotional wall, separating part of herself from the husband to whom she had promised her life. Like all such walls, this one began in a small way but grew, expanded, and became taller and stronger with the passing of time.

Ben, not unlike many young husbands, was completely clueless.

He did not realize that Sarah was walled off from him. Although both of them worked outside the home, Ben enjoyed having a wife to cook, clean, keep up the house, and share his bed. He took her out to dinner quite often—shouldn't that be proof of his love for his wife? He wasn't prowling around, chasing after other women, or shopping for an affair. He came home to Sarah, clicked on the TV, and watched auto racing.

With each passing day Sarah's emotional wall became taller and stronger. Finally, frustrated and reaching her breaking point (yet without ever having said a word to her husband about his alleged failings), Sarah told Ben that they ought to seek marriage counseling. Ben's jaw dropped. He stared at his wife as if she literally *was* from another planet. *Marriage counseling?* What was wrong with their marriage?

"We just need to talk to someone together," was Sarah's response. She did not give specifics or voice her complaints. She did make it clear that marriage counseling was absolutely necessary, in her opinion, and that the time was right now.

Ben agreed to this but privately wondered if his wife was losing her mind.

Their first attempt at finding a counselor failed miserably. Neither Ben nor Sarah felt comfortable in the presence of the woman they contacted, who was herself almost the same age as they were. Although she had a graduate degree in marriage and family therapy and came highly recommended, both decided this attempt was a nonstarter.

They tried again because Sarah insisted.

By the grace of God, the second counselor provided the sort of relaxing, no-pressure-here environment both Ben and Sarah were subconsciously seeking. It felt safe and risk-free to open up and share. Ben, who still did not know why marriage counseling was so important, obviously had little to say as the counseling session began. Greatly to his credit, he was willing to attend the session and give counseling the benefit of the doubt, just in case something useful might emerge.

With the second counselor, Sarah finally found her voice and plunged in with little hesitation. She had been stuffing these thoughts and feelings deep inside herself for a very long time, and her emotional walls were well-constructed and sturdy. Now, in the safety of a counseling office, she began expressing what she had thought and felt since the beginning of the marriage.

"Ben is just not the spiritual leader I need him to be!" Sarah practically burst out less than 20 minutes into their meeting. Even she was surprised by how much emotion her words conveyed. Clearly this was an issue she cared deeply about, even though she had never verbalized these thoughts with her husband. Now, in the safe presence of a neutral observer, Sarah's feelings came out in a rush.

Ben listened to Sarah's comments with a mixture of shock and disbelief—after all, didn't he escort his wife to church? Weren't they attending worship together almost every Sunday? Weren't they practicing Christians and Bible-believing people?

There had been no such pattern of religion or faith during Ben's childhood. By the standards of his family of origin, Ben was now a spiritual giant. He went to church, and he did so very frequently! Was there supposed to be more to it? Who could keep track of all those rules for what is required of someone spiritually?

He continued to believe that Sarah was emotionally unbalanced or perhaps mentally unwell. None of her comments made any sense.

After letting the young wife vent for a while, the counselor gently began to ask her to explain, in clear and simple detail, what the phrase "being a spiritual leader in their home" really meant to her. Sarah stammered at first, not ready with specifics, but eventually found her way to describing a small list of her deep desires:

1) Ben should lead the couple in daily devotions, at least briefly.

2) Ben should be reading his Bible on his own, just because he wanted to.

3) Ben should be attending the men's groups at church.

Given time, Sarah might have been able to develop a list of 20 characteristics of a spiritual leader according to her lifelong expectations and hopes. During their initial session of marriage counseling, she articulated the three above. Considering the shock with which Ben was reacting, three issues was more than enough as a starting place.

In as gentle a manner as possible, the counselor began asking the young wife a series of important questions. His goal was not only to coax some specifics out of the unfulfilled woman, but also to help her realize her own complicity in not having her "needs" met within the marriage.

The counselor's question cut right to the chase: "Sarah, when you've shared these kinds of requests with Ben, has he heard you? Has he started doing any of these things? Has he made a commitment to you about Bible reading or something else and then later failed to keep it?"

Sarah's face blanched as a crucial revelation struck home. Despite the depth of her feelings and the intensity of her expectations, she had never once talked to Ben about what she hoped to see. She had never asked him to lead her in daily devotions, she had never asked him to read his Bible on a regular basis, and she had never directly asked him to attend any of the men's events at their church. She had, as she recalled, occasionally pointed out to Ben an upcoming men's activity—hoping he would "take the hint," get in gear, and rush off to attend it out of sincere desire.

After much reflection, telling Ben about men's events was the only time and the only way she could recall ever speaking up about her desires. Even then, as the counselor helped her realize, her comments were not simple and direct. At no point did she say, "Ben, it would really mean a lot to me if you got involved in men's ministry and started growing spiritually." These ideas were implied by her behavior, but never stated. She was giving hints when she could and should have been providing concrete, constructive help.

Since the church wasn't sponsoring any NASCAR races, these hints were completely lost on Ben. He heard them as well-meaning suggestions, but did not understand that they came from a place deep within Sarah's picture of what a fulfilling, meaningful, godly marriage looked like. How could he have known that Sarah carried these unfulfilled hopes in her inner heart? All he knew was that his wife sometimes told him about men's events. Sitting in a marriage counselor's comfortable office, Ben was finally getting his first clues about what his wife really wanted from him.

At the same time, Sarah started to realize that mind-reading was not among Ben's personal gifts, spiritual or otherwise. As simplistic as it sounds, Sarah had not ever understood that she was storing away her disappointments and resentments instead of making simple, clearly stated requests of her husband. She began to realize that her own behavior and patterns were part of the reason Ben wasn't moving forward spiritually. She had never directly asked him to do any of these things, and she had never explained what she wanted from him.

It was a moment of highly valuable discovery for each one of them. Sarah, who had never realized the depth of her hidden anger against her husband for "not growing," began to understand that she herself might have been preventing his growth. She had never appealed to him with specific, concrete details of how he might improve or change.

She began to forgive her husband, who was not a mind-reader and literally had never understood her secret, unspoken desires for him. Ben began to hear his wife and realize he could please her by taking some relatively simple steps. No one was asking him to immediately morph into a mix of Mahatma Gandhi, Charles Wesley, and Mother Teresa! His wife just wanted him to be visibly growing in Christ.

Skipping forward to today, Ben is an active participant in a men's group at his church. A group of younger men gathers weekly to play parking-lot basketball. They stay together after playing and have devotions. The rule of the group is simple—no one can simply come and play the game; everyone must stay for the devotional content.

Ben is making a visible and meaningful change in his behavior. It helps that he enjoys basketball, but he is following the group's rule that everyone stays for devotions. He enjoys the devotions and says so. He's sweating and learning at the same time. He has invited co-workers, neighbors, and two of his cousins to attend the basketball games, and in this way he could be considered an evangelist or someone doing outreach. This is a long way forward from Sarah's picture of a husband who wasn't growing spiritually!

A bit confused and intimidated by talk about "leading daily devotions," Ben asked the counselor for some clear guidance. With Sarah present, the counselor suggested a daily devotional book for couples that is available at most Christian bookstores and is also easy to find and order online. By simply reading through the assigned chapters together, the couple could form a devotional life. Ben wouldn't have to create, write, or construct something—he would just need to turn the pages and read.

The counselor put the question directly to the young wife: "Sarah, if you and Ben are reading a daily devotional together as a habit and maybe talking together briefly about what you read, does that accomplish what you're hoping for in this category?"

Sarah happily agreed, the couple purchased the book the counselor recommended, and these days the couple is reading a daily devotion together, usually in the morning but sometimes at the supper table after they finish eating. Today it's one of the habits of this now-happier home. Reading a brief and thoughtful message gives the couple something spiritual to talk about without either having to climb a mountain, spend the weekend in a monastery, or consult a professional minister.

And Sarah does catch Ben reading his Bible at home...sometimes. "I'm really not a big reader of anything," he explains. "In general I don't read. But I'm trying to start something here. I know the Bible has a lot of wisdom, and I need wisdom, so I've been reading the Psalms and Proverbs. I can't believe how up-to-date some of these verses are—they could have been written last week."

Today Ben and Sarah live in a walls-crumbling marriage, moving together toward a future that better fits to Sarah's long-ago hopes. While it is God who so richly deserves the credit for the positive changes, it is also true that He chose to bless a process of tearing down the walls, pulling at the barriers until the deeper, truer layers of feeling were visible. Instead of hiding away in her passive sanctuary, Sarah was able to venture out into the open and express to Ben her ideas and hopes.

Unfulfilled expectations are very likely to remain exactly that—unfulfilled—until we learn how to express ourselves openly and honestly, giving our partner clear and simple explanations of how we feel and what we hope for. This is countercultural for many of us, and is perhaps best achieved—at least at first—in the presence of a trained counselor. Yet the sooner we learn to express ourselves and tell each other the truth, the sooner our walls can begin to crumble. We can learn new ways of relating that are rooted in the deep inner thoughts and dreams we often hold dear, but seldom express.

Walls Have Two Sides

Sarah and Ben's experience resembles that of Garrett and Danielle, whom we met in the first chapter. With the very best of intentions the newly married Garrett built walls around his true feelings. After the birth of his first child—a joyous occasion that even Garrett said filled him with pride and a sense of accomplishment—he began to feel that Dani was focusing her attention and her affection on their new baby. He began to feel he was being neglected in favor of a child. It didn't feel good, yet he kept his thoughts to himself, hidden away from his wife.

The arrival of their second child only intensified these feelings, which grew and expanded, hidden away behind emotional walls. Garrett didn't walk away from his wife and children—he did not abandon them or go out looking for an affair. He remained in the marriage and stayed physically close to his wife, even while keeping his heart behind the walls in ways Dani could not see and did not suspect. The result was, these walls grew thicker and higher and thus more confining. Garrett grew accustomed to living a hidden-away life, feeling neglected and at times unloved, as though he was third in line for his wife's affections, when he deeply wanted to be number one in her heart after God.

One thing these two marriages illustrate clearly is that either partner or both may be building up emotional walls and hiding behind them. Wall-building is not confined to one sex, and it's not a fault or problem on just one side of the marriage equation.

To be sure, men are often accused of failing to have feelings, failing to express them, or both. This generalization is unhelpful, but there is a measure of truth in it: Men do seem less likely to verbalize their inner thoughts and feelings than women.

Tom Hanks serves up a nice parody of this common assumption in the movie *Sleepless in Seattle.* In the living room with his brother-in-law, Tom's character begins fake-weeping over a war movie they've seen. The two men ham it up, dabbing at false tears, making fun of women getting emotional while watching chick flicks. The scene is funny and true to life, but at best it's a reflection of an incomplete and partial truth. Men are more likely to mock such feelings than to admit them.

Women are often described as being very willing to share thoughts and feelings, yet they may have been trained by their families, their culture, or both to be passive about the condition of their innermost hearts. As mentioned previously, under the guise of "submitting to their husbands" some women store up many hurt feelings and disappointments. They create a surface reality in which the marriage functions according to biblical guidelines, while at the same time there is a secret reality of deeply rooted problems. This behavior may not be conscious and chosen, because it may be conditioned by the woman's early childhood experiences, religious training, or family patterns.

There is no real merit in being passive about our feelings within our marriages. In fact, passivity may easily lead to unhealthy emotional wall-building. We are not saints when we deny what we feel, even if it seems holier to suffer in silence. Rather, the great saints on the journey of faith have been women and men of transparency and humility. We can see their doubts, their issues, and the quirks of their personalities and preconceptions. We can see the ways in which many of them are prisoners of the culture in which they were formed. They are not saints because they hide their flaws but precisely because they admit them. We perceive the struggle and the strain—it is precisely in the midst of weakness and "real life" that the power of God is most consistently seen and realized.

A Place to Begin

For Garrett and Dani, as for Sarah and Ben, the walls began to crumble in the safety provided by a counselor's office. It was the safe environment, the presence of a caring and trained counselor, and definitely the power of prayer that began to effect positive changes in these two marriage relationships.

To be sure, counseling does not always work this way. Sometimes, counseling fails. We make progress when we learn to keep moving forward in spite of failure, looking for help even if the first few helpers disappoint us.

If we own a 20-year-old Yugo and it dies along the freeway, we do not quit believing in cars. We call our parents and ask them to loan us enough money for a new Honda or Toyota. On the freeway of life, we make progress despite the setbacks inherent in piloting a used Yugo.

When a counselor does not seem useful to you, or when you're failing to connect with your minister in the way you hoped, it's not time to give up on counseling or on pastoral care. Rather, it's time to explore the advice of a different pastor or counselor, continuing your search until you find the useful counsel all of us often need.

Like the sign in the Old West saloon that reads "Please Don't Shoot the Piano Player—He's Doing the Best He Can" there is no reason to give up on counseling itself or to run down a person whose counsel does not seem helpful to you. Get up, walk out the door, head a little farther down the street, and keep looking. Good counsel is out there—keep walking.

Can some couples begin crumbling their walls without the help and guidance of a rabbi, priest, pastor, or counselor? Absolutely. Having said that, most couples need a place and a way to begin, a specific set of circumstances that create security as the process of soul-baring and wall-crumbling begins. Having a neutral but caring observer on hand to oversee our first few steps (and perhaps a few steps after that) can provide the environment in which we find our voice, confess our faults, and begin to describe our hopes. We pour out our thoughts while a referee helps us avoid offending, attacking, or harming our partner.

Quite often this is exactly where effective wall-crumbling begins.

From Hiding to Crumbling

It's clear that the problem of building emotional walls is not a "woman's problem" or a "man's problem." It is a relationship problem. Within a marriage—even a godly marriage—it can be a deadly problem. The walls that divide us and confine us to separate lives may over time have the effect of sending us outward, beyond the barriers of our marriage, to search for soul mates in all the wrong places.

Though we remain together physically, walls of protection and isolation, as we've seen, can become means to store up our disappointments, hurt feelings, anger, or unmet emotional needs as if they were treasures. We relish these inner proofs of our own nobility and virtue. Although life has been unfair to us, here we are—remaining married even though our own needs are unmet. What good examples we are! How noble it is to suffer this way and yet remain married. Our inner myth-making may deceive no one else, but it often blinds us into believing we are better, wiser, and more trustworthy than we really are.

Meanwhile in the weedy garden of our souls, bitterness and resentment put down deep roots and begin to flourish. Over time whatever beauty may have occupied our souls and spirits becomes choked out and weighed down, strangled away from future growth. Outwardly we march forward, married and apparently committed to our partner. Inwardly we die a bit more every day, falling farther and farther away from the forming image of Christ, coming far short of His wall-defying transparency and vulnerability. Others may believe the best of us, but we know better. We are faking it when we ought to be making it.

Who loses when we hide ourselves behind these types of walls?

We ourselves lose.

Our life partners lose.

Our children lose.

Everyone in our many spheres of influence may lose.

No man or woman is an island. All of us are much more connected than we realize. Although we may believe our unhappiness is invisible to others, it is more than likely that others are affected by our joyless continuance in a marriage that isn't intimate, deep, or bringing us closer together.

In safe places and at appropriate times, with determination and consistency, what we desperately need is to begin crumbling the walls, tearing down the stones, breaking the barriers that separate us from other souls and especially our spouses.

Crumbling the Walls Calls for More TV

What we greatly need is to learn new TV habits. We need transparency and vulnerability in our closest relationships so that honesty and mutual respect can grow in our inmost gardens, visible to the one we love the most. We may also need to learn to speak up, to put our wishes into words, to express our hopes and dreams to our life partner in ways that allow him or her to step up to the plate and engage in meaningful discussion.

Too often we wait for change but do not facilitate it. Too often we expect others to meet our needs without explaining how they might do so. Trapped in losses of our own making, we blame others for things we have failed to achieve ourselves. None of us are married to mind-readers in the literal sense. Most of us will need to learn how to express, explain, and explore the inner feelings we too often hide away.

Good things happen when our emotional and relational walls begin to crumble. Positive change happens within our own souls, and it flows into our primary relationships. Healing and growth spills out and begins to infect others in good ways; our example multiplies transparency and passes along infectious good germs of honesty and humility. We learn to relate to each other person-to-person instead of wall-to-wall.

The difference is invigorating...it is life-giving.

Although hiding away has made us feel comfortable within our discomfort—and although risking the disclosure of our innermost thoughts may seem more challenging than skydiving or bungee-jumping—we need to break out of the fear that holds us captive. We need to begin tearing at the walls until stones wobble and mortar cracks and we see light through the emerging holes.

We need to walk or crawl or climb in the direction of that light. As we do so it is often useful to have a guide nearby, helping us pick our way safely through the rubble and toward the truth. Such a guide may be a marriage counselor, a mentoring couple, a trusted friend, or a priest or minister. In their counsel may be the strength we need.

It will not always be counseling that saves us—sometimes counseling fails. Yet one way or another, by the grace of God, it is time to crumble some walls. Where dialogue does not now exist, monologue may be needed. Like the biblical Esther, we may need to prepare a banquet so we can speak directly to the heart of the king. Yet regardless of the pathway, the important thing is to resolve to immediately begin making progress on our journey toward intimate closeness.

Instead of waiting for our partner to rescue us from unrealized hopes, we can begin sharing our hearts and souls with each other, gently and gradually, so that the person we married can choose to become the partner of our dreams. There may be no better gift we can give than the one we most wish to receive—a life partner who is not only committed to us in a structural sense, but is bonded to us at heart…growing closer with each passing day, more known and also more knowing.

4

Busting the Ghosts

*We take every thought captive
and make it obey Christ.*

—2 Corinthians 10:5 GNT

In an ideal world, all of us would come to our wedding nights as comprehensive virgins—not just sexual virgins, but spiritual and emotional ones as well. We would not lose our hearts, our emotions, or our physical virginity along the pathway toward marriage. As two untainted souls we would join together in sacred matrimony, entering a new world of delight and pleasure with which we had had no previous experience or contact. We would be two innocents arriving in a sudden paradise.

We do not live in an ideal world.

For many of us, as we marry there are ghosts in our beds and ghosts in our heads—shards, fragments, remnants of complex former relationships that were once the source of joy and pain, pleasure, and probably guilt. Burdened by our experiences and often saddened by them, we unite in marriage and struggle to forget what has gone before. We soon discover it is difficult—it often seems impossible—to escape our own histories.

In some cases, our family and friends may believe we are virgins, although in actual fact we are sexually and emotionally tainted by years of physical bonding. We are not virgins even though we were active in our church youth group or we attended a Christian university. Previous generations neither recognize nor understand our sexualized culture, so they see in us what they expect to see: innocents getting married.

The Sexual Landscape of Today's Culture

Myopia about sexual experience seems especially prevalent among churchgoing parents with regard to their own children and teens. Church-attending parents seem unable or unwilling to believe that their own family members could be affected by a culture that is saturated with sexual images and themes. Today's adolescents are growing up in an era of sexual experimentation that begins at ever-earlier ages. Various types of sexual activity take place among teens and pre-teens while their unsuspecting religious parents are giving them lectures about avoiding drugs...never imagining the kinds of temptation their children face on a regular basis.

Such temptations are often not avoided. As we work with college-age and younger students in today's retreats, camps, and seminars, it becomes clear that many teens and pre-teens, including active churchgoers, participate in a variety of sexual experiences before they are old enough to become licensed drivers. Our culture makes them wait to operate an automobile; meanwhile their hormonal drives are being revved full throttle and allowed many forms of expression.

Even churchgoing teens may believe that if they avoid vaginal intercourse, they have not really "had sex" with anyone. Whether this belief comes from the evening news or directly from public figures, somehow it permeates today's youth culture and continually affects values, behaviors, and practices among teens.

One result is that first-marriage couples today often resemble the post-divorce remarriage couples of several decades ago. As we worked with remarriage couples then—and as we continue to do so today—this is one of the challenging issues. We confront the fact that a remarriage couple brings previous histories of sexual experience and emotional bonding into the new union—fragments of attachments and longings and memories that clutter their new bedrooms. Such ghosts are not easily exorcised. Previously married adults carry with them the memories and impressions, both good and bad, that they've gained in their prior history of relationships.

Many first-marriage couples today bring this same kind of emotional baggage. The new groom is carrying not just his bride across the threshold; he is carrying her previous sexual partners and lovers into the wedding chamber as well. Or the new bride may be giving away her carefully saved virginity to someone who has "been there, done that" not just once or twice, but with many partners over a long period of time. Gradually, marrying with prior sexual experience is becoming normative.

What Is the Church Doing?

The landscape of sexuality is radically different than in previous generations, yet our premarital and pre-remarriage counseling remains largely unchanged. As for the church at large, it clings to its fantasies: that rowdy worship times and stick-to-the-wall Velcro nights are value-changing ministry experiences for youth. Reality is much more complex. The same teens who joyously sing the praise choruses and crowd the bus to youth camp may also be sexually experimenting, hooking up in casual and temporary dalliances that litter their imagination and self-esteem with land mines. Some of these land mines are visible and some are buried below the surface, and any one of them may detonate later in life when these teens pursue serious relationships, become engaged, and join together in marriage.

Who prepares us for the future as we strain toward a marriage partnership, all the while pulling so much personal baggage behind us, weighed down by things remembered, and burdened by so many feelings of guilt, regret, and shame? Who trains us to deal with these issues wisely so we can move forward in a healthy, God-honoring marriage?

At least so far, the answer appears to be, *Not the church.* To date, the church taken as a whole is not actively involved in exploring the spiritual and moral dimensions of sexual activity before and outside of marriage. The "just say no" of prior years isn't working. Nonetheless, it hasn't been replaced with effective strategies and convincing ideas.

Parents, families, and ministry staffs are not meaningfully engaged in a culture- and value-changing dialogue—one that gives teens options to consider, virtues to think about, and compelling reasons to wait and explore their sexuality later, in the company of a committed life partner to whom they are pledged in holy marriage.

In a world dominated by MySpace, Facebook, and other social networks, the church often seems locked in previous generations both in its communication methods and also in the messages it tries to present. The church may well be presenting useful truths—let's hope so—but somehow those truths are not expressed in ways that connect with the current generation of adults-in-process. In today's culture, students in late childhood—and certainly in the pre-teen years—should receive thoughtful, wise, and useful information about what challenges they're likely to face, and how to face them.

Instead, all too often, the church remains silent. Parents genuinely believe that although such problems may be rampant in the culture, the youth group is a fortress within which sexual activity does not occur, and sexual experience is not normative. Clinging to these beliefs may provide temporary peace of mind, but in truth this view is much like that seen by an ostrich…as she sticks her head into the sand.

Although there isn't space in this chapter to build a full-orbed theology of sexuality and culture, we can and will take a look at some scriptural counsel and glean insight into useful paths for future exploration.

There's Really Nothing New…

Widespread casual sexuality was not unknown to the writers of Scripture. Where today our culture has Las Vegas, MTV, and instantly available porn via cable TV and the Internet, in New Testament times there were entire cities devoted to orgies and debauchery—places like Corinth. There it was part of a man's religious duty to have sex with the temple prostitutes. "What happens in Corinth stays in Corinth" could justifiably have been written on the gates of that city. And it would have been as patently untrue then as now.

"Do you not know," Paul writes to the Corinthians, "that he who unites himself with a prostitute is one with her in body? For it is said, 'The two will become one flesh' " (1 Corinthians 6:16—Paul is quoting Genesis 2:24). What Paul means is that a sexual union also produces an emotional bonding and a spiritual union. Paul's words point us to a metaphysical truth: Two separate bodies, occupying separate coordinates in time and space, become united in God's sight, now being "one flesh." Two human beings are bonding and becoming joined in ways they may neither intend nor understand. Even so, this bonding is absolutely real. Sexual experience, says Paul, transcends the physical world and establishes a bond that is deep and real, emotional and strong.

Where once there were two, now there is one.

As students of all things marriage and family, we continue to learn how deep and real the connections are—emotionally speaking—when two people share sexual contact. The younger the age of that contact, the more intense the bonding may be. The loss of physical virginity has impact on health and values, to be sure. Yet the resultant emotional attachment may have an even greater impact on the spiritual and personal formation of a youth.

God designed our sexuality to be an indispensable ingredient in the attachment glue that holds marriage relationships together for life. Yet instead of developing a theology that takes account of this glue, we instead treat sex as if it were more like the adhesive on a Post-It note— we may adhere here or there, but we remain able to detach, move elsewhere, and apply ourselves to another situation, leaving no mark behind. Even though we believe this and behave this way by conscious choice, traces of strong relational glue still stick to us, holding on to us emotionally and clinging to any future relationships we pursue.

Thoughts Happen: Here's What to Do About Them

Realizing the challenge described above, Paul advises us to "take every thought captive and make it obey Christ." With a wisdom that transcends cultures and reaches to our time, Paul does not advise us to "quit thinking those thoughts" or "erase your memories." Instead, acknowledging that all of us will have unwanted thoughts cross our minds and all of us will deal with memories cluttering our mental landscapes, he tells us that when this happens—as it will—the solution is to take every thought captive. He is not arguing that we can throw things forever out of our conscious memory—he is instead telling us how to deal with unwanted memories when they occur and recur.

Rather than exploring this idea in its rich biblical and theological implications (a process best reserved for sharper minds and more qualified observers), let's look at how Paul's divinely inspired strategy plays out in the daily lives of married and remarried couples as they hope for fresh intimacy while coping with past history.

Unwelcome Memories: A Frequent Companion

Celia and Don are married in a happy ceremony surrounded by many friends. Celia's two children—from her previous marriages—play significant roles in the service: dressed in extravagant and beautiful clothing they enjoy their prominence. Don's son from a previous marriage plays his guitar and sings a song during the wedding. As remarriage ceremonies go, this one is memorable, joyous, and very well done.

Don has been married once before, a relationship that lasted nearly 18 years. His divorce has been final for almost a decade, and his three children from that marriage are all adults. His youngest son, a college student, is the one whose beautiful singing voice and accomplished guitar work provide the ceremony with its best musical moments.

Celia, who is 13 years younger than Don, has been married twice before. She has one child from each husband. Both prior marriages ended before they reached their five-year anniversary. Both children are still in school and will be living with the new couple as they form a family together.

Celia's second divorce is very recent. The wedding date was actually postponed a few times as Celia and Don waited for her divorce to become final. The two are both active churchgoers, and they lived together for nearly a year before walking the aisle.*

They remain in the same house in which they were living together before the wedding. Two years into the new marriage, Celia proposes that the couple seek some counseling together, and Don is fully in agreement. They are having difficulty in the bedroom. These problems have emerged since the wedding. They ask friends at church for help in finding a marriage counselor.

> Are there solutions for such problems, or are we left to suffer the afflictions of unwanted memories and unwelcome thoughts? Is the answer more willpower, having a positive mental attitude, or bravely trying to do better? If so...there is not much hope.

Celia is the first to speak during their initial counseling session. "I can't quit thinking about him," she says, referring to her first husband. "It's not like I want to think about him—I don't. But I can't stop. And sometimes I think about him when Don and I are..."

She leaves this thought unexpressed, but its meaning is evident. Although she is doing nothing to create or produce such thoughts and feelings, her memories overwhelm her when she least desires and expects it. She feels helpless and does not know where to turn for advice on how or what to change.

As the session unfolds it becomes clear that although she has been married twice since then—to a second husband and now to Don—Celia retains a strong undercurrent of emotional attachment to her first husband. It's difficult for her to talk about this, and Don encourages her several times as the counselor works to listen and learn. Although

---

* This household type is extremely common among the previously married and divorced. Even among active churchgoers it is very typical to find previously married, divorced adults living together—in every sense—before deciding to begin a new marriage. Such adults appear to sense no disconnect between the biblical framework for marriage and their living arrangements. Once again, out theology has not even remotely caught up with addressing patterns of behavior in our culture.

Celia raises the issue in regard to sex, there are complexities of value and meaning attached to these recurring experiences.

"I don't want to go back to him," she insists. "The divorce was the right thing. My life is better now, everything is better now. I don't want to go back to him and I wouldn't go back to him, even if he begged me to." Celia appears to be fully sincere. She has moved on, and she isn't interested in going back.

Celia's first husband is remarried and has several children with his current wife. She interacts with him once or twice a week since they share custody of their young son from the marriage. Celia tells her counselor that these interactions are not remotely romantic or flirtatious in nature. For the most part, they are about logistics: picking up their son, dropping him off, making plans. The two ex-spouses also talk about how he is doing in school and how well he is adjusting to bouncing back and forth between two homes and two families.

There are many layers of complexity and challenge woven into this ex-spousal relationship. The son they share bears a strong physical resemblance to his biological father. Every time Celia looks at her son, she sees her first husband looking at her through his eyes. Some of her son's gestures and facial expressions exactly resemble ways in which Celia's first husband looks or moves.

Celia thus remains connected with a whole file of memories and visible reminders of the physical appearance of her ex-husband. She is flustered about this but has no clue how to move past it. Should she quit loving her son, quit being around him, try to quit looking at him, or hope he quits looking so much like his dad? It's impossible to do these things anyway, she believes.

Celia makes it very clear—she is making no effort to hold on to her first husband or reconstruct her original marriage. It's the furthest thing from what she wants. She is focused on moving forward. Yet despite what her brain consciously processes and believes to be true, the ghost of her first husband is always hovering around the borders of her current life.

"I don't want him back, but I can't get rid of him," Celia says later in the session. "It's like he keeps coming into my brain sometimes, especially when I'm with Don sexually. I don't try to think about him, it's just that…"

Don is paying attention, holding hands with his wife, staying surprisingly calm. Obviously he's heard Celia talk through all of this before. Just as obviously, though, he is concerned about it and looking for answers he doesn't have.

Are there solutions for such problems, or are we left to suffer the afflictions of unwanted memories and unwelcome thoughts? Is the answer more willpower, having a positive mental attitude, or bravely trying to do better? If so…there is not much hope.

At times well-intentioned people believe that counselors are or can be miracle workers. However, counselors are not so gifted after all. It is God who works miracles, God alone. Yet sometimes counselors get to have a very good seat in the arena as God displays His power and creative work in the midst of the complicated lives we lead and the difficult traps we encounter while trying to survive in today's culture.

Advice Given, Advice Taken

The counselor quotes the passage from the apostle Paul about taking every though captive, and together they all talk about how it might apply to the new marriage. Both Celia and Don can see why the Scripture might be useful, but what does it mean? How does it work in real life?

The counselor's applications are simple and practical. "First of all, both of you should pray on a regular basis that Celia can be free of these kinds of thoughts and memories," he recommends. "The fact that both of you are asking God for this will help unite you together as a couple. We can be certain that God hears our prayers. And God does not just *hear* when His children pray to him, He also *answers* their prayers."

Can prayer alone prevent unhelpful thoughts from occurring or take away our memories of past relationships? Certainly yes—this is always a possible outcome when we seek help from an amazing and miracle-working God. There are no limits to God's power and ability, and He Himself decides how and when He will act when His children pray.

There are times when simple faith produces simple results: immediate and drastic changes that defy all other explanations and flow to us from God's grace. More typically, however, God's work in such cases is direct, tangible…and gradual. Often He chooses to leave our memories in place yet limit their power over us. He gives us grace to deal with our uninvited thoughts and ideas, helping us conquer them with His presence and His help.

As time passes and the work of God's Spirit progresses in our lives, we are able to deal with these unwanted or unpleasant memories without losing our balance, without descending into depression or despair, and without falling back into our former patterns and habits. God partners with us in powerful progress. The more time passes, the more these thoughts and patterns decrease, and the more His power is visible in every aspect of our lives, including how we think, speak, and act.

Just as our bodies create new physical cells while the old cells die off, in the same way God puts new spiritual energy within us. We are constantly being renewed from within; He brings us increasing levels of release and freedom.

One reason that older, more mature spiritual mentors often seem so positive and encouraging is that they have lived a long time under this ongoing influence, being re-created by the Spirit of God, conforming more closely to His divine image. Earlier in their lives, many of them faced the same types of battles and challenges that we face. By walking consistently in the same direction and by forming new habits and practices with the help of God's Spirit, these seeming saints are living freer and fuller lives. This is not because they've never been tempted or never had times of struggle, but because they've emerged from the struggle with a clear sense of God's presence, God's power, and God's promises.

We'll talk more about re-creation in the next part of this book because it's a vital and essential process if we want to reach toward spiritual depth and intimacy in our marriage relationships. We'll explore the pathway of re-creation and look at examples as it happens within relationships.

Meanwhile, Celia's question brings our attention back to today and right now: "Can God take away these thoughts I'm having so I never have them again? That's what I want, more than anything."

With regard to unwelcome thoughts, it's worth repeating that God can instantly cause us to never again have certain types of memories, just as He might deliver a middle-aged man with a lifelong habit of swearing so that he never again curses, not even when he's surprised or angry. God is not boxed in by our boundaries or our limited understanding of His works. He is all-powerful, and all things are possible with Him.

However, the usual pattern of His work seems to be that He builds small daily victories in us, limiting our unwanted thoughts or reducing our outbursts of swearing or helping us resist the negative habit or behavior we are trying to change. Many of us do not experience an instant or sudden deliverance that lasts for a lifetime.

Instead, many of us walk the journey of life with a new partner—God—who is bringing us new victory, changing the way we see the world around us, and changing the person we see in the mirror every day. These changes are definite, concrete, and real. They are also gradual and ongoing, rather than sudden and all-inclusive.

Accordingly, even though both Celia and Don will be praying for her immediate deliverance and relief, the counselor offers suggestions in case Celia's thoughts recur. The advice varies depending on when and how Celia's thoughts form, and it is tailored to the types of situations she commonly encounters.

"If you do have an unhelpful thought about your ex-husband in the bedroom, stop right then and breathe a prayer asking God to take that thought out of your mind and remove it from you," he advises Celia. "You do not have to pray out loud—and it's probably best not to, in that moment. Clearly, God hears your prayer when you voice it in your head, and saying it out loud is not necessary."

The next step, the counselor suggests, is to immediately find a "replacement thought" and to focus on it as intensely as possible. When Celia's mind is invaded with an unwanted memory or an unhelpful thought, he advises her to take a further action step: Fill her imagination with something else that replaces what is unwanted.

"When you are in bed with Don," the counselor continues, "if you should accidentally have a thought of your former husband, after a quick prayer, refocus your entire attention on Don. Pay very close attention to him: his appearance, his breathing, his nearness, his pleasure. In other words, while you ask God to remove the unwanted thought, focus your attention and all of your thoughts on the caring, wonderful husband who is with you at that moment."

What about seeing reminders of her ex when Celia looks at her son? Is there any hope for getting past these recurring DNA-inspired memories of her former husband?

The counselor is specific. "First of all, pray about that also," he says. "Beyond that, when you find yourself catching glimpses of your ex in your son's facial expressions or mannerisms, stop right then and breathe a prayer for your ex-husband. If he's away from God right now, pray for his salvation. If he's right with God, pray for his spiritual growth. Instead of running away from these reminders of him, stop a minute and pray that God will be at work in his life.

"You don't need to linger over these prayers." The counselor smiles. "You don't need to start a prayer meeting. Just say a quick prayer asking for God's help or blessing on his life. As you do this, it will become much less of a burden to be reminded of your ex-husband when you see him in your son—now, if it happens, it's a reminder to pray. Among other outcomes, this is going to result in a whole lot of prayers being said for your ex-husband, and that alone is a powerful and positive thing!"

There is nothing sensational or new in any of these suggestions.

They are merely some practical contemporary applications of ideas that were voiced by the apostle Paul nearly two millennia ago. Paul has similar ideas in view when he advises his readers in Rome to "not be conformed to this world, but be transformed by the renewal of your minds" (Romans 12:2). As we saw earlier, Paul's world was much like our own: cosmopolitan, urbane, sophisticated, filled with sexual temptations, and often flooded with moral decay. Paul writes to believers who were struggling with exactly the kinds of issues that today's followers of Christ are likely to confront.

Again, though we might wish our transformations would be sudden and surgical like a brain transplant operation, in practice most meaningful transformations seem to occur gradually and eventually, taking place over a period of time. There is a long and steady progress in the same direction, aided by God's divine power and help.

"Habit is habit," Mark Twain writes, "and not thrown out the window by any man, but gently led downstairs step by step." Twain is a better counselor than he knows. The more normative human experience is that God comes alongside us in our battles against habits or addictions or negative patterns. He joins with our efforts and helps us start succeeding where we have often failed.

This is not a matter of our own willpower; it is the presence of God's Holy Spirit within us. Yet God often waits for our will to be clear. Because He grants us enormous latitude and freedom, His help arrives once we are serious and determined and ready for change. Prior to genuine repentance and turning away from past habits, God graciously waits for our decision. As we make that decision He joins our battles and begins winning them for us, with us, and through us. This pattern accurately describes most of the cases we see and observe as counselors, as God invades challenges with His strong help. As we cooperate with Him, as we repent of past attitudes and behaviors, He works in us to achieve new victories and to reform us as new creations.

We are morphing into something different and better, and most probably this transformation will play out over months or years. In the same way that it takes time to learn how to ice-skate, or become an electrical engineer, or bake a perfect pie crust, often our progress is gradual and inconsistent rather than immediate and effortless. If you watched over the last decade or so, you discovered the world figure-skating championships that all those years of practice paid off for Michelle Kwan. On her way to those rinks, however, she fell down a lot.

Unless she spends time fantasizing about her ex-husband or dreaming about getting back together with him, Celia does not need to "repent" of having unwanted thoughts attack her mind at unhelpful times. But trying to go in two directions at once will not work. She cannot fantasize about her ex-husband at some times, dwelling on such thoughts and lingering over them—and then wish those thoughts didn't suddenly form in her brain at other times. Such a divided effort is sure to fail.

Fortunately, this is not her situation. She is not consciously indulging in or treasuring any wrongful ideas about her ex. She is a happily remarried woman who wants to be free. She wants to get rid of the ghosts in her bedroom…and her kitchen, her dining room, and her backyard. Given the chance to work in Celia's life, God can immediately and permanently remove all her thoughts and memories of her ex-husband—God is God—or He can daily bless Celia and Don as they pray together, asking for His help, moving forward toward peace and freedom.

Since we cannot know in advance how God will choose to work, the best we can do is place ourselves in the position where He can do anything He wants to do in us—and then watch and learn as He displays His power in His way.

Six months later Celia is excited by the changes in her thought life. "It's better!" she insists brightly during a follow-up session.

The counselor, faith-filled but skeptical by nature, asks a few questions. "Celia," he begins. "It's okay to tell the truth here. If the problem has gotten worse, it's okay to admit that. If the problem is very much the same, just say so. Or if the problem has truly gotten better, that's fine too. But whatever is going on, let's be honest in this room and face life exactly as it is."

Fortunately, Celia does not sense this remark as an attack on her character. "It's so much better!" she says again, smiling. At her side, Don nods his head in approval and agreement.

"We've been praying about it together," she continues. "And I've been doing the things you suggested when I think about my first husband. Everything is better already. I don't have those thoughts very much anymore. And when I do have thoughts like that, they don't last very long. Everything is better now, including in our bedroom." She blushes.

Words on paper do not capture the joyous nature of Celia's confession, nor do they capture the wide grin spreading across Don's face. Clearly this couple is moving forward in positive directions, experiencing meaningful change in their relationship.

On a daily basis and in brand-new ways, Celia and Don are happily remarried.

Ghosts in the Bedroom: Passionate Pictures

A thousand miles away, Erik is marrying a pastor's daughter.

Erik is a new believer. His commitment to faith began five years after college, and before then he looked, sounded, and acted just like the culture around him. He was immersed in sexual activity, chemical experimentation, and casual, throwaway relationships. He is unable to count his previous sex partners, and he estimates it's beyond the dozens and probably in the hundreds. He literally doesn't know.

After accepting Christ and beginning to attend church, Erik begins a friendship with the daughter of his pastor. This friendship blossoms into romance but proceeds slowly and prayerfully. Because of his past, he's careful about physical expressions of love and is very guarded in how he conducts the new relationship.

To be certain, Erik's carefulness is aided by the pastor's protective nature. Less than thrilled when Erik shows interest in his daughter, the pastor is gradually won over by the young man's consistent behavior and sincere desire to do the right thing. Now time has passed and it's clear to everyone that Erik and Mina are serious about honoring God. Erik's new life in Christ seems genuine and real, and it is. With the blessing of both families, one Christian and one highly secular, he and Mina are married—in her father's church. The wedding is well-attended and the new couple receives almost every item they registered for. Life is good.

Yet six months into their marriage, Erik and Mina seek counseling. On the surface they seem very compatible and much in love. They share the same hopes and dreams for the future. They aren't fighting or quarreling or having trouble making wise decisions. Instead, their problems are private and reflect a fairly common occurrence when one or both partners has prior sexual experience. The problem involves ghosts in the bedroom.

"When I am making love to Mina," Erik says candidly and in a relaxed way, "these sudden pictures or thoughts about other people keep popping into my head. That's always been true before, too— when I was having sex with one person, a memory from someone else might cross my mind. It never bothered me before. Now, in my new life and in my marriage—I don't know how to say it—it feels like this is wrong somehow. So I want God to take away these thoughts and these pictures about other people."

Mina looks at the counselor but does not speak.

Carefully and prayerfully, the counselor begins processing Erik's statements and working toward some common understandings. He shares much of the advice and counsel that was given to Celia and Don, although in a condensed and much simpler form. As the session unfolds, the counselor feels divinely inspired to ask Erik a further question. The counselor is uncomfortable with its content, but he prays and decides to act on it anyway. (Usually, he refers sex issues to other therapists.)

"Erik, I have a question for you," the counselor begins. "It's kind of personal, so if it's too personal please say so. You don't have to answer this."

"Just ask me," Erik replies bluntly. "Don't worry about it."

The counselor hesitates, breathes a prayer, and plunges forward.

"Erik, when you are having sex with Mina, are your eyes usually closed or are your eyes usually open?" The counselor is staring intently at a sheaf of papers laying on the desk in front of him.

Erik's answer is immediate.

"Closed," he says. "Always."

The counselor leaves space for silence in the room, then returns to the theme of the divine prompting he believes he's received.

"Erik, here's what I'd like you to try," the counselor advises. "I'd like you to try keeping your eyes open when you and Mina are together. I'd like you to try watching her, looking at her, studying her, noticing the changes in her breathing or her expressions.

"If you catch yourself closing your eyes, open them back up again. Blink and get back to looking at your wife. Study her. Memorize her. Drink in every detail of her."

Erik's face contorts in a quizzical grimace. "I'm not sure I can do that," he says softly, contemplatively.

Mina speaks for only the second or third time in this lengthy session. "Can you try?" she asks her husband, grabbing his hand and holding it. "Can you at least try?" Her request does not have the tone of nagging or pushing. Instead, it seems fragile and almost shy.

He shrugs his shoulders and gives a long low sigh.

"I can try." He shrugs. "I guess I can try."

Six weeks later the counselor sees Erik and Mina at a conference. In this highly public setting, he won't ask the couple any marriage-related questions.

However, they have no such reservations or qualms.

"Guess what?" Erik says as he sees the counselor.

The counselor does not reply, leaving the young husband to answer his own inquiry.

"It works," he says, smiling widely like a kid.

The public nature of the setting does not allow for detailed follow-up questions. "Do you mean…" the counselor asks.

"Yes, exactly," Erik says, still grinning and obviously elated. "That problem we talked to you about is completely gone. When my eyes are open I do not have thoughts or pictures or anything else. All I deal with is what my eyes are seeing!"

Beside him, Mina squeezes his hand. Her eyes brighten. "Thank you," she says. "Our times together are much better!"

Her face is blushing beet-red. She looks down at the floor. Other people are walking past during the conversation, but it is impossible for them know the true nature of the chat even if they overhear a few words.

Erik beams with obvious pride and a fresh level of self-confidence. "It is much better," he says. "Thank you."

"That specific bit of wisdom really came down from God while we were talking together," the counselor tells the glad couple. "That isn't something I've ever shared with anyone else before—although now maybe I will. That was just a God-thing."

The couple hears this remark but doesn't seem to care. Mina blushing and Erik beaming, the two insist that the counselor realize one thing more than all else, which they carefully stress: "It is better."

Working *with* God's Design, Not Against It

Celia and Don are a remarried couple, each with extensive prior histories. Many miles away, Erik and Mina are a first marriage, but Erik brings with him a lifetime of sexual experimentation and too many partnerings to count. So despite the fact that these two couples are beginning new lives that share little in common in terms of detail and content, the common ground is that both desire some "ghost-busting." Both couples are in need of help; they admit this and search for a useful counselor or minister or friend.

They are taking the right steps: acknowledging the problem, talking together about the problem, then moving forward to seek counsel and advice from appropriate and knowledgeable sources.

More Than Procreation and Recreation

What we have seen in the lives of Celia and Don, and Erik and Mina, reinforces one of the deep realities about the sexual nature in all of us—we really do bond and connect during the act of sex. Even if we make no effort to meaningfully connect, even if we don't remember names, even if there was never a relationship by any standard but only a quick hookup—even in such cases, bonding does occur. We cannot prevent it by claiming indifference or trying to be callous and aloof.

This truth transcends the whole debate about procreation and recreation. For many centuries a repressed church maintained that the purpose of sex was procreation. If you went into the bedroom, it was because you were there to make babies. This is why God gave us sexuality, the church proclaimed—so babies could be born. There was an implied and sometimes even open suggestion that sexual activity between married partners was "dirty" or "earthy"—but nonetheless married couples were obligated to have sex anyway. Since children needed to be born, sexual partnering was a necessary evil to keep the planet populated.

Times change.

Today there are Christian sex manuals that are far more graphic than secular books on the topic were just a few years ago. Today within the church there are many voices celebrating sex as recreation: fun and games for married couples. This long overdue reaction to centuries of attempted repression is normal and natural. It also contains much truth—God does design us to experience this kind of joy, and to enjoy experiencing it!

Yet something else is at work in our sexuality. It is not physical, but emotional and spiritual. It is a bonding, a connecting, an establishing of rapport between souls that takes place even when it is not acknowledged or understood. Sex is relational glue; it is meant to be. This is one of the most compelling reasons to save sexuality for marriage, where God's design is to build a lifelong, committed, "together for always" couple.

The principles illustrated in the situations of the two couples in this chapter have been tested and tried by many others, both in remarriage and original marriage. Couples of all ages have wrestled with unwanted ghosts from the past. They have discovered it is possible to make meaningful, measurable, positive progress in this struggle to bust their ghosts and cleanse the atmosphere in a new union. Across more than two decades of counseling we have watched God change many such struggles into ongoing and consistent successes.

We do not need to abandon hope. We do not need to wrestle forever with our unhelpful memories or our thoughts. Instead we can offer ourselves to God, asking Him to bring us the release and relief we so greatly need. He may do so instantly and permanently: He has done this, and He may choose to do this again at any time.

Or God may do so gradually but strongly, moving us forward through a series of learning and growing times that bring us into a new life full of new strength and victory. In either case, whether His help and hope deliver us instantly or gradually, the key is that we are moving forward in healthy directions, embraced by His grace, filled with certainty that there are better days ahead, and that new life is possible.

This chapter's applications of Paul's advice to "take every thought captive" have been field-tested in homes across North America and beyond, and many couples are now living testimonies to the effectiveness of scriptural counsel. These strategies really do bust the ghosts, in the bedroom and elsewhere. Yet the main thing to remember as you read and apply these principles is that you are not relying on strategies, techniques, or methods alone. Nor are you simply building up your own willpower or practicing mind control. Instead, you are inviting God to help you change your own or your partner's thought life, imagination, and memories, freeing you from the power of unwanted images and unhelpful ideas. You are engaged in an essentially spiritual practice, and you are seeking God's spiritual participation in your relationship.

When you are doing TV—practicing transparency and vulnerability—it is appropriate and meaningful to share your struggles of this type with the one you love the most. It is not always necessary to discuss these matters down to the specific details (and you may be wiser to avoid giving too much detail or describing your thoughts or impressions too specifically), but a general discussion helps clear the air and move you on in your spiritual progress together, rather than separately. Progress in these often difficult areas is rightly the work of God. The good news is this: *God works.*

⌒

With consistent movement in the right direction, instances of ghosts in the bedroom can and do become fewer and farther between. Memories may occasionally plague you, yet you'll notice that such memories no longer seem to have the same emotional force they once had.

Your life is freer, your relationship is fuller, and the mutual progress you've made in exorcising ghosts from your marriage bed has actually become another source of a satisfying and pleasant sexual union.

Sex was God's idea in the first place. Beyond its design for procreation, sexuality is intended for recreation—and it is intended to be the relational glue that holds couples together despite all the challenges of building a lasting, committed relationship. As you work in this direction you will find a welcome freedom in the ever-expanding dimensions of God's power and grace, delivered from struggles and raised to new levels of living, loving, and enjoying marriage.

5

Dying to Self

When Christ calls a man,
he bids him come and die.

—Dietrich Bonhoeffer

I remember you told me this would be really difficult," Marcus says slowly, facing me across a small table at a crowded Starbucks where we've agreed to meet for coffee and conversation. "But I never knew it would be this tough."

Beside us a busy group of young moms chats noisily, babies in strollers pushed up beside their table. To the other side of us an earnest real-estate agent is selling, selling, selling—insisting to his listener that "this is not a down market, this is a terrific buyer's opportunity!" Both Marcus and I try to suppress a smile; if this isn't a down market for real estate, what is? Home prices are tanking, mortgage rates are rising, and foreclosures are becoming more common every day. A down market? By any indications, that's exactly what this is.

However, Marcus has invited me here to talk about his marriage, and he's buying the coffee. Six months ago I performed his wedding at a large contemporary church in the upper Midwest. Although I didn't know his bride before their pre-marriage counseling began, I've known Marcus most of his life. He's a firmly committed Christian, a deep thinker, and a serious student of philosophy, contemporary culture, and the emerging church movement. I like him—he's a God-seeker and he's absolutely real. There's little pretense in him.

He takes a slow sip of his tall caramel macchiato, triple shot. He seems to be preparing himself for our conversation.

"What I've figured out is this: The problem in my marriage is me," he tells me bluntly and directly. "We're getting along okay, we're not fighting, there aren't any big 'issues' we need help with. But what I'm learning from my marriage so far is that I'm the one who is stubborn. I'm the one who is immature and basically selfish."

"Marcus," I tell him, leaning back in my chair, "I already knew you were a guy."

A smile spreads across the intense face of my 28-year-old friend. He relaxes, and some of the tension immediately eases out of him. Throughout his life Marcus has tended to take everything too seriously. Disciplined and demanding, he's a good student and a quick learner. He tends to fall below his own expectations of himself, which are sky-high. A child who never seemed able to please his birth father despite trying so very hard, he grew up with strong perfectionist tendencies. He's still got them.

We talk, guy to guy. It's a free-flowing conversation unheard by those around us, busy with their lives, their families, and in some cases their potential futures in real estate and home mortgages.

Marcus pours out a litany of sharp self-criticism. He gives me example after example of the small, daily, frustrating ways in which he is selfish, stubborn, or unwise. And he's right. His self-diagnosis is entirely correct. What he doesn't realize is that he's accurately describing the behavior of almost every young husband, almost every newly married man in North America and perhaps beyond.

We've been learning about marriages and families for more than two decades, and our research has taken us to all 50 states, 11 of Canada's provinces, and about three dozen other nations, including most of Europe. Thus, although Marcus doesn't realize it, he is not just summing up the state of newly married men—he is also capably describing the patterns shared by many men married for years—men who tend to remain immature and selfish even within the context of long-term, outwardly successful marriage unions. Some of these men have saints for wives, but they are not worthy of their long-suffering spouses.

Meanwhile, Marcus is just a normal man—not more, not less. What we mean is, he cares about Marcus more than he cares about others, including the woman to whom he has pledged his life and his heart. He didn't realize how self-oriented and self-focused he was while he was single. It took a short stroll down a candlelit aisle before he began recognizing that he is selfish, much less mature than he thought he was, and not a very good listener.

Welcome to manhood, young husband!

While selfishness and immaturity are not specific to one sex or the other, we'll begin this chapter with a frank discussion of male selfishness within the context of a new marriage. This can be a major problem, especially within some Christian marriages, even more so in conservative homes that hold to a theological conviction that the man should be the undisputed ruler of the house. In such places, as Lord Acton observed more than a hundred years ago, "Power tends to corrupt and absolute power corrupts absolutely."

Marcus, who would never endorse the man being lord and ruler over the home in the literal, paternalistic sense, is frustrated by the surprising emergence of his inner boss. Where did it come from? Why wasn't he expecting this? A mere six months into his Christ-centered marriage he is already realizing that he likes to have things his way; he likes to win arguments rather than lose them.

Somehow these patterns were not yet evident during their courtship. Blinded by a dizzying emotional attraction to each other, both Marcus and his future bride lived at a high level of cooperation. Their interaction with each other was usually courteous, self-sacrificing, gentle, and kind. These behaviors are not at all abnormal during courtship—yet somehow they often fade away after a bride and groom are united in holy matrimony.

Even during pre-marriage counseling such couples may represent their relationship as stress-free, mutually cooperative, and relatively low in conflict. What this actually means is that one or both parties are repressing their selfishness, stubbornness, or both in the interest of building and causing the relationship to grow. Once the union has been formalized, especially as time passes and newness wears off, the self-focus of the groom, the bride, or both will begin to emerge and affect the daily dynamics of the marriage relationship.

Marcus describes his conversations with his wife. By his own confession he has already proved to be short-tempered, irritable, impatient, and hard to live with. So far, he tells me, his wife is gently and graciously deflecting his tirades rather than fighting back. So Marcus isn't angry or upset with his new bride—instead he's extremely disappointed with his own conduct in the new marriage. He isn't living up to his image of himself. The man he sees in the mirror is not the Marcus he believed himself to be.

"I'm terrible! I'm hurting the person I most want to show my love to," Marcus blurts out at one point in our conversation. I glance around the busy coffee shop. No one is paying attention to us. No one seems to be eavesdropping on this highly caffeinated chat. The animated table of young moms is making so much noise that no one nearby could possibly hear us anyway.

"I find myself yelling at her a lot," he continues. "I can't believe how often my volume level creeps up there, and all of a sudden I'm shouting at her. I keep showing her what she's doing wrong, how she needs to improve. I'm acting like I'm a drill sergeant in the army and she's a brand-new recruit. Worse than that, I'm treating her like a *stupid* recruit. Where did all of this come from, anyway? This isn't me!"

Marcus is not abusing his wife physically or sexually. However, as he himself confesses during our lengthy interaction, he may be harming her verbally and perhaps also emotionally. Despite his best efforts to be humble and patient, Marcus finds himself correcting his wife, giving her instructions about how she ought to be doing many of the household tasks, and generally ordering his married life as if it involved himself alone. By his own description, he spends a lot of time making sure things get done his way, trying to change the way his wife performs even the simple, everyday chores.

Where Did This Come From? This Isn't Who I Am!

None of these are tendencies Marcus saw in himself in college or during the years after college as he experimented with graduate school, overseas volunteer missions, and a few short-lived careers. It is the arena of marriage that suddenly reveals to him that he tends to go into battle too often, fight over the wrong issues, and speak to his wife with a wrong attitude.

Surprised and ashamed by these discoveries, his first instinct is to seek counseling from a trusted friend. He recognizes he needs to become a much different person around the house—a much better lover for a godly woman who simply wants to be valued, affirmed, and celebrated.

"I love her, I really do," Marcus says softly later. "But if you followed me around the house, and if you listened to what I say to her and how I say it, and if you saw how much I insist on getting my own way—I sure don't act like I love her a lot of the time."

In other words, thank God there's no YouTube camera in the house!

The skills Marcus needs to learn do not come naturally for most men. Wired to explore, conquer, and achieve, men tend to dominate in their marriage relationships without even being aware of it. They don't actually take classes in how to be selfish.

In general, men are wired that way. And while not all men are perfectionists or as attentive to detail as Marcus is, men tend to live by the hamburger-chain motto: "Have it your way." When they can't get quick compliance at home, some men bark loudly, some become abusive physically, and some lose interest in their partner and begin looking elsewhere for compliant companionship. What men don't tend to do in those settings, generally speaking, is learn to humble themselves and lead by serving.

Ruling by Force vs. Leading by Serving

As the manic fury of Adolf Hitler spread throughout Germany and Nazi soldiers began invading neighboring nations, people of good conscience debated their ethical choices. Is it morally acceptable to use force if you can prevent much future evil? Are there times when holy, righteous, upright people must reluctantly resort to force and violence in order to prevent something far worse from happening?

This debate is as old as time. Entire movements, such as the Quakers and the Mennonites, have decided that peaceful living is the mandate of Scripture. These God-followers are opposed to war and decline to see the holiness in the phrase *holy war,* viewing that idea as an oxymoron. These groups have a long record of pacifism that speaks powerfully to the consistent integrity of their views.

In the intense film *The Mission,* a priest faces this dilemma in a remote tropical jungle. Working to improve the physical lives and to accomplish the spiritual salvation of indigenous people, he discovers these tribal groups are being exterminated by enemies. Motivated by his love for the people, the priest agonizes over whether or not he will fight to save them or passively allow evil to triumph. Suddenly this is not a philosophical discussion but a question from real life: What should be done when evil is at the door, well-armed and ready to do immediate harm to the innocent?

A thoughtful young Lutheran pastor in Germany wrestled with these same issues, not as mere theology or intriguing philosophy but as a daily reality in his home country. Although Hitler's original law-and-order platform resonated well with many everyday Germans, and although political and economic life in the country improved for a season, there were evil undertones even among the earliest activities of the rising Hitler.

Bonhoeffer was deeply troubled. How should he preach to his congregation during such a time? What should he say to them, and how should he say it? What should he advise them to do as their country fell victim to a madman, and as entire groups of people began to be singled out for persecution, forced removal, and the death camps? Although the true extent of Hitler's horrors was neither known nor knowable, enough reliable information reached the young pastor that he recognized evil when he saw it. Bonhoeffer's worries were not just about how to preach to others—he also struggled with what he himself should be doing to oppose the increasing fury of the anti-Semitic leader.

Ultimately he decided to join a group that was exploring ways to eliminate Hitler—and thus hopefully return Germany to decency and order. The plot was soon uncovered, and Bonhoeffer was arrested, imprisoned, put on trial, and then killed by hanging. He died young, no less sincere in his faith than the Quakers; no less a Bible scholar than his brethren among the Mennonites. Bonhoeffer's choice was to take action and attempt, as much as he possibly could, to oppose and eliminate evil at its source.

Before his untimely death at the end of a hangman's noose, Dietrich Bonhoeffer gave contemporary Christianity a priceless gift: several volumes of thoughtful, perceptive theological reflection and inquiry. In his books such as *Life Together* and *The Cost of Discipleship,* Bonhoeffer explores what it means to follow Christ, and what it will cost us if we are serious about becoming Christlike in our obedience to the faith.

A passage from *The Cost of Discipleship* opened this chapter, a quote I first wove into a wedding homily for my good friends DeAnna and Jon. Since conducting their service I've gone back to Bonhoeffer for a few other weddings as well. His wise observations, as spiritual and theological truths, apply beautifully to life within a marriage relationship.

"When Christ calls a man, he bids him come and die," Bonhoeffer observes. Here he is not inviting us to commit suicide. Instead he is accurately revealing that following Christ means a genuine, cut-to-the-core death to our inner self: death to our natural selfishness, death to our vanity and pride, death to our insistence that our own needs be met and that things be done our way. Perhaps the single best piece of pre-marriage advice you can ever receive is this: As you marry, die to your selfishness.

This death is not to identity or personal worth. Instead, it is a death to a self-oriented worldview that tends to value others only as they give us what we want, when we want it, in ways we deem useful and helpful. This is the kind of death our marriages so desperately need from us—a death that liberates us from our self-orientation.

Come and die, Bonhoeffer says. Why is this dying to self so difficult for most of us?

If you believe in the natural goodness of all people, volunteer for a few Sundays in the two- or three-year-olds ministry of your local church. Spend an hour or so shepherding children who are just emerging into language skills and a more conscious although greatly limited understanding of the world around them. What word is among the first you'll hear during your observations?

"Mine!"

Children learn this word quickly and practice it frequently. Before they can verbalize they can push, pull, tug, pout, scream, cry, and throw a fit. They will defend their territory, their blanket, their nook, their baby doll—whatever the object is, they are clearly able to decide it's their own possession. They stake a visible and angry claim to ownership, defending their turf against all invaders.

"Mine!"

It's the cry of a new husband also, or perhaps a long-married one. He wants life his way, by his rules. If he's biblically trained he may believe this is his divine right because the man is the head of the household. He tells himself he's not abusive—he certainly would never be a petty tyrant—he's just carrying out his God-given duty to lead.

He wants things his way. Right now.

A Contemporary Husband, or a Timeless Throwback?

Marcus discovers these same tendencies in himself, and he's genuinely shocked. "This isn't me at all," he wants to protest. "I'm an enlightened, liberated, twenty-first-century kind of guy. What do you take me for, some kind of caveman?"

He is surprised and embarrassed to discover how selfish he is. This sudden discovery is accelerated by his entering into marriage. Sharing his daily space and his personal possessions with someone else helps Marcus identify his inner two-year-old. Marriage is like that—we learn more about ourselves in the first six months than we may have learned in the entire two or three decades leading up to our wedding vows.

Marcus—peace-loving, thoughtful, reflective Marcus—has discovered a selfish inner nature he never knew existed. It has taken him only a few months since walking the aisle and promising to "love, honor, and cherish." Penitent and hoping for sincere change, he is looking for answers.

The counsel of Bonhoeffer will resonate within attentive husbands like Marcus. How do we put this counsel into daily practice in a marriage? How do we not only recognize our selfish tendencies but begin to move past them and behave differently? Like other men in his position, Marcus is not asking a counselor to help change his wife's behavior. He realizes he is his own stumbling block and his own major problem.

Humble Servants and Servant Leaders

Against this backdrop the model and instruction of Philippians 2 is useful training for all new husbands. Before learning along with the good people at Philippi, let's remind ourselves of the oft-quoted lesson explained in Ephesians 5:23: "A husband has authority over his wife just as Christ has authority over the church" (GNT).

Lest we are tempted to quit reading, the passage rushes us forward quickly. In verse 25, we're instructed in this way: "Husbands, love your wives just as Christ loved the church and gave his life for it" (GNT). Somehow this second key emphasis is not always heard with the same intensity as the first component (verse 23).

Textually speaking, we barely have time to begin celebrating the authority and lordship of the husband before Paul moves on to describe how love operates in that role of authority: "…just as Christ loved the church and gave his life for it."

> Rather than ruling with an iron fist and insisting on being first over all others, Christ instead humbles Himself, grabs a basin and a towel, and washes feet. Christ is modeling groom-behavior and teaching us a lesson in being husbands.

An eloquent passage in Philippians 2 fleshes out that kind of love in human terms. Having all power and all authority, Christ humbles Himself and takes the role of a servant, bending low to meet the needs of those around Him. He does not use or abuse His power, position, or title; instead He reaches for a basin and towel, serving others in the lowest and humblest way possible.

"He was humble and walked the path of obedience all the way to death—his death on the cross," Paul tells us in Philippians 2:8. This staggering truth shatters our illusions of grandeur, dashing our hopes of building an empire in our own living rooms. Christ—who has all authority—bends low, takes the role of a servant, and lives out humility.

Those who choose to love their wives just as Christ loved the church now have a clear example to follow. It is not the military model of high commanders and low soldiers, it is not the corporate model of high CEOs and low employees, it is not the barnyard model of the proud rooster strutting around in the dirt. No, this is a different model. The dirt in the Christian model sticks to the garments of the simple servant as he washes, heals, mends, and cares. The dirt in the Christian model washes off the feet of those who are being served. It is carried away in a bowl, to be emptied out elsewhere.

This is the servant leadership prescribed by Scripture and described as the way in which Christ as bridegroom loves His church (we His people) as bride. Rather than ruling with an iron fist and insisting on being first over all others, Christ instead humbles Himself, grabs a basin and a towel, and washes feet. Christ is modeling groom-behavior and teaching us a lesson in being husbands.

It's a lesson we may not want to learn, but it's a lesson we definitely need.

Servanthood Is a Choice

Servanthood is a marriage lesson for both genders to explore, not just men. Though we've opened this chapter with a man's perspective, it is useful and important for both men and women to confront their selfish focus and begin to make needed changes.

While Marcus was surprised by the emergence of his inner boss, Corinne learned the scary implications of her inner princess—again, not until she got married. Before her marriage to Jeff, Corinne was blissfully unaware of her self-focused life and world.

"My mom was 39 when she got pregnant with me, and Dad was four years older than that," Corinne tells us in an early meeting. "So by the time I reached my teen years, my parents were in their fifties already. They were mellow and easy. I know I was supposed to be fighting with them all the time, but that just never happened for us."

An only child, Corinne was favored by her father with all kinds of gifts and attention, cherished and appreciated by a mother who was delighted to finally bear a child so comparatively late in life. Feeling incredibly loved by both parents, Corinne never realized that she didn't grow up learning how to compromise, sacrifice, or think about other people and their needs.

"My dad bought me a light-blue Mustang for my sixteenth birthday party," Corinne confesses to us with a wide smile. "It was the perfect car! Exactly what I'd always wanted. But somehow I never understood how unusual that was—though I had friends from large families, I didn't know how rare it was to get such expensive gifts. I thought most kids got cars from their parents when they learned how to drive. Both of my parents were always buying me things—my mom would buy me shoes and purses, my dad would buy me a new computer. Both of them treated me like the center of their entire world."

Corinne should have been able to read the truth on her shirts.

She had two different shirts, one pink and one white, that were both emblazoned with an accurate name for her tendencies: "Princess."

"My dad still calls me that." Corinne blushes. "And I kind of like it."

Turning more serious, she begins to tell us that it has taken her nearly three years of marriage to realize how selfish she is, how rarely she thinks about Jeff's needs and wants and point of view. By God's grace, the princess may be growing up.

"God has really blessed me," Corinne admits. "I went from a family in which I was the star attraction and the center of attention, right into a marriage in which my husband just thinks the whole world revolves around me. I have it great in my marriage and I know that, I really do."

It isn't conflict that has Corinne turning thoughtful and open to some new learning—instead, it's good preaching.

"Living in Pheonix, I attend Christ's Church of the Valley," she says to us. "And lately the pastor has been talking to us about what it means to follow Jesus with our whole hearts. And the more I hear about that, the more I realize I'm not like that—it's not who I am at home. It's not who I am in my marriage.

"But you know what? Jeff is like that. My daddy is like that." She gets quiet. "What I need to learn," she tells us, diagnosing her own case, "is how to think about Jeff more, how to really figure out who he is inside. I need to quit letting him spoil me so much, and I need to start spoiling him for a change..."

No one raises any argument here.

Good preaching has motivated useful change in a newly married young woman. Instead of berating her for being selfish or accusing her of being a bad wife, a minister is simply holding up a powerful example for her to see: Christ humble, Christ serving, Christ loving. This young wife can look at Christ's example and make her own application of truth as she realizes, *That's who I need to be.* Sometimes the most powerful sermon applications are the ones we make ourselves as we listen, pray, and reflect on the truth of the message.

Whether you are a wife or a husband, dying to self means honoring your partner and serving your spouse with a glad heart, acting in humility and love, giving up the starring role so that someone else can shine through your life and through your marriage. It means putting someone else first, letting someone else be prince or princess while you wash the laundry, feed the dog, or care for the children. It's a lesser role, not the place we're accustomed to in our self-oriented, me-first culture. It's humility, and we are born to pride, selfishness, and apathy toward others.

For Corinne, the days ahead will be spent in learning some new patterns. She may continue to be spoiled by a loving husband, but meanwhile she will be doing her best to also spoil him, voluntarily taking lesser roles and doing undesirable chores. Like Goldie Hawn's character in the popular movie *Overboard,* Corinne will move from a life of pampered luxury into the daily grind of serving, helping, and honoring others.

It's a change all of us need to make, sooner rather than later.

Dying to Self: A Brief Instruction Manual

Dying to self is a thousand little choices we make every day.

It is thinking about someone else as you rise and begin your morning. It is smiling at someone and helping to start their day on a cheerful, positive, encouraging note.

It is praying for someone throughout the day instead of wondering whether anyone is praying about you and remembering your challenges.

Dying to self is about making extra efforts, even when you have less energy.

It is coming home tired from work, but choosing to serve and comfort someone else who is also tired instead of putting your feet up and waiting for a foot massage.

It is cheering up your partner instead of wishing someone would encourage you.

Dying to self is about forgoing all those arguments over "whose turn it is."

It is changing the diaper or getting up for the feeding or even carrying out the trash or putting away the dishes. It's a lot of little things: choices we make when all we want to do is sit down and relax, maybe read the paper, maybe watch some television.

Dying to self is like that—it is daily, and it's about the small stuff.

Couples who go the distance learn the value of sweating the small stuff. They realize that most of life is not dramatic, intense, and life-changing. Instead, most of life is daily, petty, and potentially annoying. Life has amazingly few cross-country road trips with good friends, all expenses paid, seeing this beautiful country of ours. Life has quite a lot of traffic jams and road construction as we commute to work. Life is full of rude and incompetent drivers cutting us off in traffic or stealing our intended parking spot.

Couples that go the distance learn this and know it. Though they may take a few getaway trips from time to time and these may be health-restoring times of rest and renewal, successful married couples recognize that life is lived daily on a small scale.

Small-scale selfishness destroys the foundations of a relationship every day, eating away at the unity and affection that hold a couple together. Yet small-scale servanthood has just the opposite effect—building personal attachment and marital unity and helping relieve the stress and struggles of everyday life.

There is enormous relational power in this small-scale servanthood. We begin to bless another person through our humility, our attention, our valuable help, and most of all through our prayers. Whether we are praised for these actions, or even if we sometimes feel taken for granted, the truth is that we are blessing our life partner in ways that are literally life-changing for marriages and relationships.

One reason that small-scale servanthood is so effective as a daily habit is that all of us deal with so many sources of stress in our marriages. There is never enough money, there are frequent health challenges, the future of our job is uncertain or perhaps we lose it due to downsizing or a corporate buyout. Meanwhile we often feel like we're failing as parents, falling short of our hopes and dreams, or settling into a routine that will prevent us from ever living the life we always wanted.

In the midst of these daily stresses and setbacks, when someone loves us, cares about us, and serves us, we are renewed and reborn. We begin to look at life differently and we begin to smile more often, laugh more loudly, and appreciate the value of simple everyday life in a family—just as it is, not as it may become.

Servanthood is not about spotlights, drumrolls, and winning awards. On the contrary, it is a life lived in small-scale focus: *How can I help you right now? How can I bless you this day? How can I pray for you as you drive off for yet another job interview, losing your confidence and wondering if we'll be able to hang on to our home?*

Small-scale servanthood notices the details. That is where it truly shines.

Dying to Self Is Not Becoming a Doormat

Dying to self is not about stifling your own opinions, keeping your frustrations bottled up inside of you, or learning a passive style of relating to your life partner. It's not about being indecisive when faced with trivial choices like where to eat dinner. Although these things may appear to be unselfish on the surface, instead they often lead to future conflict and potential disaster.

Many married adults have opinions on various topics but have never learned healthy ways to express them. As time goes by, these patterns are reinforced by life experiences. Passivity breeds passivity, yet this has nothing at all to do with dying to self.

Most of the physically abusive husbands we've worked with fit the same mold. They are mild-mannered men who live for long periods of time in circumstances that upset them: Their kids are out of control, their houses are messy, their wives are spending too much money and running up huge debts. Physically abusive men tend to see all these things happening around them and become very upset, yet they fail to respond and communicate and work toward effective change. They do not learn how to openly and honestly express their feelings and bring about new circumstances. Instead they remain silent on the outside while boiling away on the inside, which is a prescription for disaster. Unable to process and vent their emotions, these men do their best to keep the lid on their feelings...but you know an explosion is coming. The only question is when.

This type of husband is storing away anger and resentment and bitterness. This is like a pot of water boiling on a stove, with the lid firmly clamped on the pot. Sooner or later there's going to be a major mess—the lid flies off and people get burned. Although this is largely a male pattern, there are passive wives who erupt in this same way, becoming violent toward their husbands or others around them.

Some spouses learn how to manipulate this process to their own advantage. They turn up the heat as the passive partner simmers away in silence. And they keep turning up the heat until finally they get what they're looking for—a big explosion. Dysfunction in a relationship is rarely one-sided; most often both parties contribute behaviors and patterns that lead to harmful and even disastrous outcomes.

Do these foolish spouses deserve what they get? Of course not. Physical violence and abusive behavior is never warranted, regardless of the situation. Yet the law of cause and effect is steadily at work in these partnerships. Some adults know how to trigger or cause the effect of being harmed by their partners. For whatever reason—they need sympathy? they want to play the role of martyrs?—some married persons deliberately trigger the very violence they then complain about after they run to safety in the comfort of friends. These seeming victims are actually largely in control of what violence reaches them, in what form and at what times. Further study would be useful here, not to justify or perpetuate domestic violence but to help reduce it as much as possible.

Dying to self is not about covering over your anger with a lid of passivity. It is not about denying your feelings or pretending to be okay when you're not. Ironically, behaviors of this type may actually be very selfish. The patterns may raise your self-esteem by allowing you to believe the lie that you are more holy, more mature, or more spiritual than your partner. After all, you aren't complaining! What an example you are!

Rather, dying to self is a choice made by a healthy person, someone who openly expresses thoughts and feelings within the context of a marriage. Instead of pretending not to be angry or acting as if all is well, a healthy person learns how to openly express thoughts, opinions, attitudes, and values. Going forward, that same healthy person learns how to give and take, how to compromise, and also when to stand firm and hold out for a choice or a value that matters very deeply or is hugely important. Healthy people express their values—so that when the heat of life gets turned up, the steam can boil off rather than building up under a lid of pseudo-holiness. Healthy people don't often explode, because they've learned not to try to keep all that pressure bottled up inside them.

Changing Our Lifelong Patterns

A man may remain passive at home because his father did the same. A woman may learn to keep her feelings bottled up inside because she believes she should "submit to her husband." In either case these unhealthy patterns have nothing to do with dying to self. Healthy marriages exist around TV—when two partners are open, honest, expressive, and self-revealing, each in his or her way, without hiding or holding back, without pretending or storing away resentments.

Neither the husband nor the wife is called by Scripture to stifle emotions, deny feelings, or repress inner thoughts and values. Such behaviors are not prescribed by the Bible and are not healthy for marriages and family relationships.

Nor are we called to become doormats, using "dying to self" as an excuse for letting others manipulate, abuse, or harm us or others.

Nothing in Scripture's words about the husband's leadership empowers him to abuse his wife, dominate her, or control her every choice. Nor does Scripture excuse him for doing so. As we have already observed, the husband does have a calling—it is to humble himself, take on the role of a servant, and love his wife the way Christ loves the church.

Wives who adopt patterns of outward submission while seething with inner pain or anger seem to misunderstand Scripture and miss its true intent. Any such wives who are reading this book must understand—here and now—that by "dying to self" we do not mean allowing someone to walk all over you at any time and in any way. These are not healthy behavior patterns for anyone, wife or husband. There is a vast difference between becoming a doormat to be walked on by others—and making a conscious choice to humbly wash someone else's feet as a gift of love.

Christ in Focus

Jesus was no doormat—not at any point in His life and ministry. But He did, in the company of those He loved and as a gesture of humility and compassion, kneel and wash the dirty feet of His closest friends. In so doing He was not allowing them to abuse Him or permitting them to destroy His identity or personhood. Instead, as a truly free person, He was choosing an intentional act of humility—a liberating act of service and love.

We do not follow His example by choosing passive–aggressive behavior patterns. We do not follow His example by repressing our thoughts and feelings or by trying to keep a lid on our rage as we boil up inside. We do not follow His example if we allow anyone, especially our life partner, to reduce us to a subhuman level by dominating us and attempting to control every aspect of our lives.

We follow Christ's example as we express our emotions in healthy ways, allowing our inner feelings to be heard and known. We follow His example as we value others enough to let them see and know who we really are, inside and out. We follow His example by intentionally choosing a life of humility.

It was Christ's own choice to give up the privileges and perquisites of His high station, step out of the limousine, and begin to serve the simple daily needs of ordinary people. Where He found blindness, He gave sight. Where He found hunger, He broke bread and provided food. Where He found illness, He spoke blessings and provided health. These miracles did not take place among the rich and the powerful (most of the time) but rather among the weak and the poor. Though He could have ignored such people, He displayed a deeper and fundamental truth: All of us are weak and all of us are poor.

When we help the least of these—and when we do simple acts of helping and serving within our marriages and families—we are honoring Christ and following Him.

A Study in Contrasts

Living for self is rolling over and feigning sleep when the baby cries, hoping your partner will eventually wake up, get out of bed, and take care of the problem. She probably will; meanwhile you snore loudly and hope she believes you're sleeping.

Dying to self is getting up gently, trying not to wake your partner, and making your way to the baby's crib so you can warm up a bottle, clean up some fresh poop, or calm and comfort your child. You don't keep track of this. You don't put a notch on your bedpost or a check mark on your notepad every time you're heroic and sacrificial. You just get up and do it...quietly, gently, because it's needed and because someone must.

Do you get a medal for this? Yes—but not in this present life.

Living for self is pretending that dishes wash themselves, shirts iron themselves, grass cuts itself, oil changes itself, and groceries restock themselves in the refrigerator. Living for self is easy—it mostly involves a radical denial of how things happen day to day in a busy household. Have you ever thought much about that?

Dying to self is a bit more difficult. Dying to self is looking around one day and realizing that your mommy is five states away. If the floor needs scrubbing, you grab a mop. If the dishwasher needs filling, you load it and start it. Dying for self doesn't insist on keeping score, taking turns, or dividing tasks. These strategies may be helpful in some ways and at some times, but often they only serve to reinforce the self.

Saying to someone else, "It's your turn," is the self's way of defending itself against sacrifice and unpleasantness. Taking turns is just one more way of measuring a relationship to see who is giving more than the other. Such measurement isn't helpful.

What's helpful is two people serving each other, giving to each other, not waiting for applause or recognition but simply living out small-scale servanthood in the nursery, kitchen, garage, and around the house.

Living for self is pretending that "guy time" is absolutely essential to your life, that a few minutes at a bar or several hours playing golf are exactly what you need to be and become a better person. You stop off for a drink on the way home from work. You look for ways to be out of the house, getting your "guy time" and having fun. All guys do this, probably more than you do, so you reason to yourself.

Dying to self means being home when the kids are fussy, or when the house is a mess, when there's fighting and mayhem and the noise of children in every square inch of your residence. Dying to self means that instead of escaping, you graciously sit down with your wife and offer *her* some time away from the kids.

"Why don't you go see a movie?" you suggest to your spouse.

"Could you use a little 'you time' today?" you may ask her.

Instead of dodging the tedious work of managing noisy young kids, dying to self means choosing to stay home and learning how to do that work yourself. Why? So your partner, who may well do most of it on a regular basis, receives some valuable moments of time away to rest and be refreshed, shop or dine, see a movie, get a haircut, or go have coffee with a friend.

Dying to self is hard. If it weren't hard, more people would be doing it.

Dying to self involves seeing yourself in the mirror as you really are, in ways you may never have seen yourself before. It means admitting that even though you're a nice person, you're also someone who cares about yourself first, others later. You bring this behavior and these values right into your new marriage relationship. You aren't the flawless hero of your previous self-image; you are a flawed and selfish person: a human being.

If you're a man, "Love your wife just as Christ loved the church" may be the highest calling and most difficult assignment you ever receive as a husband.

It is also one of the most powerful relationship-builders you will ever encounter. When two married partners, in healthy and appropriate ways, both learn to die to self and serve the other—this is the beginning of relational greatness. The power of servanthood starts strong, but it builds exponentially when both partners embrace the understanding that marriage is about giving, not receiving. There is an upward surge in satisfaction levels that fills both partners with inner contentment.

Each marriage will differ in terms of roles and patterns, gifts and graces. Some marriages are places where the woman of the house makes many of the daily decisions, including most or all of the financial choices. In other relationships these same functions are done by the husband, with the wife's consent and advice. Yet regardless of roles and patterns, the concept of mutual servanthood explodes into relationships with power and with much-needed grace, taking us to brand-new places and to relational fulfillment.

We can summarize it this way: Greatness happens in marriage relationships, but usually there are one or two deaths involved. Greatness happens, but usually it doesn't happen automatically, quickly, or easily.

Instead, one or both partners begin to realize that humble sacrifice is the key to fostering a lifelong companionship, one that's filled with knowing and being known.

Relational greatness is difficult and takes time. The pathway to relational greatness is about small-scale servanthood, which over time becomes a natural and normal part of your daily life and even your identity. In a household formed by two effective and genuine small-scale servants, relational greatness is almost unavoidable.

So how do we move forward toward a stronger union?

We look in the mirror and see ourselves accurately, as Marcus did after only six months of being married. We listen to a sermon and hear ways we need to change, as Corinne did while attending weekend worship. For the first time but hopefully not the last, we begin to see ourselves as we really are: selfish and too often focused on our own happiness, our own wishes, our own comfort.

We begin to make changes. Rather than radically rearranging every aspect of our daily lives, instead—in small ways and simple ones—we begin pulling more of the load and honoring our partner rather than seeking comfort and help for ourselves. We do so because the powerful example of Christ is always before us, calling us to step out of the lofty place and assume the humble role of a voluntary servant.

Dietrich Bonhoeffer's clarifying call echoes out to us as we try to deconstruct our unhealthy habits and establish new and vital life-giving patterns, one step at a time.

He echoes Christ: "Come and die."

part three:

re/creation

re/creation:
renewing and growing,
imagining and producing new ideas,
patterns, and ways of being;
the process of being made new

6

Birthing the Real

...I had wings, and dreams could soar,
I just don't feel like flying anymore.

—FROM "EVERY NEW DAY" BY FIVE IRON FRENZY

One way or another, relationships begin as attraction.

The attraction may open as a one-sided story. He likes her, so he carefully studies how to approach her. He begins a friendship with her, and then he successfully takes the friendship to the next level. Or maybe she discovers him—she flirts with him but he doesn't seem to notice. Tired of waiting around, she calls him and invites him out on a date. When the attraction first begins, often only one person is aware of it and ready to explore what it may mean for the future.

Sometimes attraction remains a one-sided force that never grows or develops into something mutual and interactive. At other times attraction builds in an uneven way until eventually both parties bond and connect with similar strength and mutual commitment. Regardless of the later process and outcome, when a new relationship begins, the levels of attraction may be radically different between the two parties. One of the persons may not feel or sense any attraction whatsoever.

"I like you as a friend," she may tell a guy she's dated, "but that's all." She is attracted to him, but she thinks of this attraction in an almost brotherly way, well-suited for a close and meaningful friendship. On his side, whether he verbalizes it or not (he might be wise to wait for a while to express this particular thought) he may see her much differently: as a potential romantic interest and someone he'd like to date, court, and possibly even marry.

Many males manage to hear the phrase "I like you as a friend" as the kiss of death. It's simply a closed door, a lost opportunity, or a slap in the face. In their view, they are being rejected for romance and considered for something that—in their opinion—is at a much lower level and worth a lot less. It's like applying for a new job as a bank vice president and being told, "You have a great portfolio—and we happen to need a new security guard right now. We'd like to hire you to patrol our parking lot. When can you start?"

Kind of a mixed blessing.

In a similar way, many females manage to hear the phrase "I'm not ready to make a commitment right now" as some form of rejection of their attractiveness, compatibility, or desirability. In reality, such a statement may either be an accurate observation made by a reasonable, mature person, or simply a way of avoiding responsibility and remaining immature. (Immature men are not an unknown cultural phenomenon.) In any event, "I'm not ready" is not in and of itself a statement of rejection. It may mean a variety of things, including "Let's keep this going and see what happens."

Setting the Backdrop

Men and women who are wise understand that relationships which begin as friendships can move in unexpected directions. To be certain, some relationships that begin as friendships will always remain so: compatible friendships. Yet many of the committed long-term married couples we've worked with tell us a different story. What began for them as "just friendship" turned into a lasting romance neither of them expected.

We call this "romance by surprise."

"We started out as friends," Nicole says. "And for a long time I don't think either one of us was even considering marriage. Somehow we just grew closer and closer, until I couldn't imagine trying to live my life without him."

Beside her, Gary nods his agreement. "I was totally happy with it as just a friendship," he remembers. "And I'm not sure I can tell you when it changed, but it did."

Friendship is often a great springboard to later romance. When love does bloom, it springs up in the midst of a relationship that may already be mutual, self-sacrificing, and beneficial for both parties. Love blooms well in this type of soil.

When romance grows as it should, two mature individuals begin to forge a lifelong friendship that is based on mutual respect, shared values, and compatible temperaments. Each one gladly makes sacrifices for the good of the other, and each one strives to help the other become the very best person he or she can be. This kind of mutual sacrifice characterizes long-term, highly satisfied married couples—they look out for each other, support each other, speak well of each other, and build each other up.

Building each other up is not about ignoring each other's defects of character or imperfections of behavior. Instead there is a level of honesty unmatched in most or all other types of relationships. Committed for life, two people can tell each other the truth, speaking this truth in love, with the clear goal of moving each other toward the pattern and model of Christ. They can birth the real, unashamed and unafraid.

Two mature partners are transparent with each other, not hiding from the light but stepping into it so as to be fully seen and fully known. Two mature partners are also vulnerable with each other, in the privacy of their own relationship, accepting the risks of becoming known as part of the process of growing together in love.

Instead of being the enemy of romance, realism becomes its greatest friend. Puppy love grows up: Self-sacrifice and deep levels of commitment take its place. This is why older couples, farther along on the road to personal maturity, often have the kind of marriages we so greatly admire. For a long time, each has been blessing the other, building up the other, believing in the other, staying true to the other.

The Blessings of Steady Togetherness

Over a period of many years, this steady progress moves the relationship to higher and higher levels of unity and satisfaction. Couples that experienced a fair amount of stress and dissonance in their early years of marriage may find conflicts diminishing or even seeming to vanish altogether as time passes.

"We'd have to look back more than 20 years to find a serious fight or a strong conflict between us," one happily married couple reports. "Looking back, it seems like we decided to do all our fighting in the first three years and get it over with!"

As the couple learned to adjust and became skilled at resolving conflict and making sacrifices for each other, the relationship grew deeper and much more serene. Adults who describe their relationships in this way are often among the most well-adjusted and fulfilled persons we encounter.

The mature adults in these couples tend to know what each other is thinking. They're on the same page as they experience community life, the broader culture, and simpler things like church services and music concerts. They laugh at the same jokes and share a wealth of memories, treasured forever. These couples are enjoying a rich harvest of unity and peace after many seasons of planting, watering, weeding, and tending their relationship. Harvest is a beautiful season. It catches many of us later in life, but there are some who reach it sooner than others.

These blessings are within reach for all of us as married persons, yet some couples may find the journey takes more than just the first three years. All of us, even early in our relational journey, are intended to be soul mates and heart companions. Though we may express this in a wide variety of ways based on our culture, our family of origin, or our chosen personal style, the truth is, we are created for intimacy. Nothing less satisfies us. Deep in our hearts we know that more is not only possible but is in fact the intention of forming such a close and lasting relationship.

We know, as we begin our marriage walk together, that the journey is intended by God to lead to places of deep inner connection and lasting love. When such connections fail to take place, and when love wanes instead of growing, we may tire of the existing relationship and begin to think about, or perhaps pursue, other partners.

This is where we go wrong. We are too quick to start over, attempt to erase our personal histories, and believe we can find happiness by jumping into a different bed or starting down a new road with a new person. We aren't created this way. Instead, we're built to bond for life and to experience fulfillment within the context of keeping our promises.

Fulfillment is not about starting over with a new partner, but about journeying together with our current spouse toward the good things God has in store for all of His children—a deeper and stronger intimacy and a fuller love than any we have ever known.

Going the Distance: Passing into History?

Across contemporary culture we can't help noticing that romance often fades, attraction dims, and relationships end. The primary model for contemporary families may well be brokenness: separation and divorce. The landscape of family life is filled with remarriages and blended families, striking out and starting over. Several generations have come of age in a world where intact birth families are increasingly rare. In fact, stepfamilies are already the predominant family type of the twenty-first century within the United States.

Against this backdrop we continue to research why some marriage relationships beat the odds, go the distance, and last for a lifetime. Our process involves studying the healthy habits and best practices of married adults, paying special attention to married couples who report a high level of satisfaction and fulfillment. What can we learn from these contemporary success stories? What are these marriages doing right?

Among other variables, one significant fact emerges: Successful long-term marriages are very good at *birthing the real*. That is, these relationships are places where two mature adults bring a high level of self-awareness into the marriage, and then go on from self-awareness to a realistic, reasonable, clear-eyed view of the relationship itself. These couples risk more, give more…and ultimately receive more.

Birthing the real is about knowing yourself, seeing clearly, and growing up.

Birthing the Real: The Role of Age and Maturity

One reason so many marriages end quickly is that contemporary adults tend to marry too young. This has nothing to do with chronological age. There is nothing inherently wrong with a 16-year-old woman or a 19-year-old man. You probably know people at or near these ages who are wiser and more mature than persons twice their chronological age.

The "too young" problem is about the fact that many people marry before they really understand who they are as persons. Not knowing themselves well or accurately, they are in no position to understand what kind of a person they need as a marriage partner—someone who will balance and complement them, helping them achieve maturity and depth. They rush into a relationship not even knowing themselves, and thus unable to recognize a compatible life partner within the field of potential mates.

We call this "the blind marrying the blind." Unable to see who they really are as persons, people marry early and marry unwisely. They choose the wrong temperament, wrong personality, or wrong mix of character traits. They marry in a rush of hormones or in the flush of intense emotional fever. They act without reason and often contrary to it. The result is a relationship that contains one or more immature persons. This is a formula for severe struggles and possibly also a breakup.

When the marriage later explodes, the immature may look around for excuses, blaming everything and everyone else around them. They blame their partner for not loving them or not behaving well. They blame their families for rushing them into marriage, even if the families were not directly involved. Most people who experience the sudden and swift end of a marriage dig up many factors. But they fail to go looking for answers where it really counts: What aspects of my own behavior, attitudes, and personal immaturity helped cause this relationship to end? This question too often goes unasked.

One reason we're encouraged about today's remarriage couples is that many of them marry later in life, not just in chronological age but in terms of personal maturity. Thus they do a much better job of choosing a life partner. Although you'll hear widely quoted statistics showing that remarriages fail at a high rate (60 percent within five years, as much as 75 percent in ten years), these statistics tell an incomplete story. The deeper truth is, when couples remarry at or above age 30, their odds of having a lifelong marriage increase dramatically. The hidden secret behind the terrible statistics for remarriage is that early-age remarriages are crushing down the overall percentages. When you remarry at 21 or 22 years of age, you may well still be too young to know yourself and be able to wisely choose a compatible life partner. (This same factor wrecks the odds for original marriages as well.)

To beat the odds and go the distance in our marriage unions, should we all wait until we're at least 31 years old before we marry? Statistically, it's worth considering. Practically speaking, it's mostly irrelevant. The issue is not how many days you've been alive, but whether you've spent those days learning about who you are as a person. You've been busy growing older, but have you actually done the hard work of growing up and becoming mature? Is it accurate to consider you a grown-up by now?

Today, it's not surprising at all when households contain no mature adults. This is the primary reason marriages end, whether they're a first or a fifth marriage. This is also a factor in the high divorce rate of some states in the southern U.S. where couples tend to marry at earlier ages, often with full parental consent and agreement.

We are marrying too young—before we've done the difficult work of learning who we are, recognizing our true identity and also our limitations.

Growing Up: The Work We All Must Do

Growing up is about birthing the real, getting a good handle on that person in the mirror, understanding who you are and how you got that way. Why do you do things the way you do? Given a certain set of circumstances, how will you respond and why?

For a long time we've looked at families of origin as significant factors in pre-marriage counseling. This is wise and good practice, but incomplete. Regardless of our family history and our experience within family life, ultimately we ourselves must come of age. We must grow up, put the past behind us, and decide who we're going to be as persons. Moving beyond trivial questions like fault and blame, we begin taking full responsibility for our own emotions, our own attitudes, our own behaviors, and our own choices. We begin birthing the real—understanding who we are and what we truly need. For most of us, this means facing a reality that may be harsh and unflattering, but this is a necessary step forward if we're ever going to become healthy, grown-up adults.

Our friends often know the truth about us, but they may be too polite to inform us of areas of weakness that they plainly see in our lives. Or we may be so immature that we choose to surround ourselves with weak friends, those who will never stand up to us and never imply we're in the wrong or need to change.

As an illustration, one church leader, secure in his identity and confident of his own gifts, may hire staff members who are excellent and who have some gifts exceeding his own. This leader may seek feedback from others, constantly trying to improve his skills and refine and enhance what he does as a leader. He knows he's good; He wants to get better.

Another church leader, much less secure, may prefer to hire staff members who are mostly younger, less experienced, and less capable—so his own inadequacies are less visible. Insecure and unsure of his own giftings, this leader always tries to look better than those around him. He fears his failings and may avoid much-needed growth.

If we're going to grow up, we need reliable mirrors and courageous friends. We need to have access to people who will speak the truth into our lives, showing us things we should quit doing, things we should start doing, and things we can do a lot better. This counsel may be unpleasant and difficult to receive—and it may also be exactly what we need to hear.

My Life with Mirrors

If you want to watch a woman frown at herself, buy her a mirror.

This works with almost any woman, including the strikingly beautiful ones. Even my wife and coauthor, the most beautiful woman I (David) know, will often look at her reflection in the mirror and express dissatisfaction. I find myself wishing she could see herself the way I—and all who know her—see her.

In a small way I also helped raise three beautiful women, something that should not be stressed too much. These women have none of my DNA, and among the three of them they have several very much alive birth parents who should receive much more credit for their many good qualities. The presence of these women within our own family circle and our sphere of influence was relatively brief in some cases, but lengthy and meaningful enough that they call me "Dad" and always send me Father's Day cards (which are among my favorite unmerited gifts to receive).

So when it comes to dwelling in a house full of women, or camping outdoors in a tent full of women—or if the question is about navigating across the country for thousands of miles with a minivan full of women—then I should be something of an expert by now. Which means, as is the case with most men, that I know nothing at all about women…or at least nothing very useful.

I do know that mirrors make women frown. Personally I believe almost every woman is attractive—it's just that most of them don't realize it. Most women compare themselves to anorexic supermodels, somehow seeing the models as more appealing. Apparently, many women intuitively believe that most men, or perhaps all of us, are allured by stick figures with sneering faces.

This is simply not true.

Art directors are attracted to women like this, as are fashion designers. Real men generally prefer real women, not the starving ones. Yet somehow many women in North America and Western Europe are conditioned to believe that beyond-skinny is the only acceptable body type for females. Does this make sense to anyone?

Mirrors make women frown.

But the reality is, I frown when I look in a mirror too, and I'm not a woman. I grew up frowning at that adolescent face in the mirror, that gangly, spindly-looking guy who wasn't exactly a future movie star. He wore thick eyeglasses, and he looked like he probably spent all his time studying.

Which he did.

He spent the rest of his time frowning into the mirror, wondering when he would grow facial hair, why he had his first gray hair at age 16, and whether or not he would end up starting to lose his hair in his thirties.

Which he also did.

These days, that same guy looks in the mirror and wonders where all his hair went. I see him there, worrying about his hair.

He often frowns.

The Great Reversal

Most of us grow up frowning into mirrors. Then we become adults and realize we shouldn't look in the mirror much. There's no point—it will only end in frustration.

Eventually we relax and accept ourselves as we are, which is something Californians seem to do better than others. I love living in California because if I don't want to dress up, or if I'm not having a good hair day, I can go to church or go shopping or go out to eat and no one—or at least no one local—is going to judge me on the basis of external appearances. Californians are in the dictionary under "laid back," and they do not judge a person by clothing or hair or surface details. Anything goes—including at church.

I can't prove this because I don't have the relevant data, but I am pretty sure that if a Californian is going in for a job interview, he wears sandals. This is how you know whether the guys in line at In-N-Out Burger have job interviews later that day. If they're wearing sandals, you know they're between opportunities and making applications.

Otherwise they're running around barefoot, mon.

We need to learn the physics of mirrors, which is fairly simple.

When you look in a mirror, everything is reversed.

So the prideful woman who looks in a mirror and sees beauty is deceived. And the rest of us, men or women, who look in the mirror and see someone who is unattractive and unacceptable—we are also deceived. We are seeing a reverse image—we are not seeing an accurate reflection of our true worth and value.

We May Not See Our Faults Accurately, Either

Unfortunately this same principle is true when we look in a mirror metaphorically and examine our personal character rather than our outward appearance. Somehow, we can look in a visible mirror and see the flaws in our appearance, magnifying these into blights that prevent relationships from forming. Yet at the same time we can attempt to examine our character by looking in an invisible mirror and completely miss seeing the flaws in our thoughts, attitudes, values, or behavior. These defects and imperfections actually may be tragedies waiting to detonate.

Whether we are literally looking into a mirror and frowning at our own face, or whether we are figuratively looking into a mirror and assessing our own character, we are seeing reverse images. We may look and look again, but we are usually not getting a good handle on how things are. We are not yet birthing the real.

I was in college before I realized that most of us don't know ourselves. For a while now I've been a card-carrying member of the chronological adult category, and the same thing holds true in this club. Most of us have no clue who we really are.

It is remarkable that a man or woman can graduate high school, do some vo-tech training or go to college, obtain a good-paying job, get married, and become a new parent, yet still be mostly clueless about his or her own personal identity. How is this possible? How can a person navigate some of the major decisions of life and yet never begin to chart a course toward maturity, personal integrity, and spiritual growth?

As a child you believe teens are mature—until you reach that age. Then you may believe university students are mature—until you move into the dorm. You may look around at married people and think of them as grown-ups. Then one day you're sitting around a room filled with married people and no one seems to have learned much of anything. And on it goes. People can turn 40 or face 50 and not yet know themselves and not have learned how to delay gratification, sacrifice for others, or be responsible. The aging process is a physical reality, but it may not yield maturity or good sense.

A World Without Grown-Ups

Ending a marriage is not so much about falling victim to lust issues or having a wandering eye. Splitting up is rarely about upgrading one's life partner and hooking up with someone who is more beautiful, fresher, or more interesting. These things do happen, but they are not the essential factors in most broken relationships we witness and work with.

Much of the time, divorce occurs because one or both partners are still children themselves—a fact reflected in the choices and decisions they make and the unrealistic way they view the world around them.

Often, divorce occurs because a man and a woman can be emotional adolescents well into their thirties or forties or later. Divorce happens because a reasonably mature and even confident woman can decide to marry a "project male" who never grows up. Divorce happens because even a mother will abandon her children in pursuit of pleasure, affirmation, her vanishing youth or appearance, or some other gaping void in her life—a void that exists primarily because she has never managed to grow up and become a fully functioning adult in a society that desperately needs more of these.

Divorce occurs because accountability, personal responsibility, and commitment are adult values, and many married people have never learned to become adults. They still haven't birthed the real. They look in the mirror, but they do not see themselves as they are.

In contrast, the presence of mature adults in a society, regardless of their marital status, is a pathway to social greatness and a more equitable world. Mature adults care about others and make decisions with altruism and compassion. Mature adults improve our world.

Mature adults cast their votes in elections and make decisions based on an informed view of the world around them. Mature adults defer some possessions and opportunities because they realize that achieving these status symbols too soon will involve high levels of debt and perhaps perpetual obligation to lenders and credit card companies.

Mature adults provide the steady guidance and moral compass that the larger culture needs in order to flourish, thrive, and perpetuate itself. But where will we find such persons in a culture that chases eternal youth?

Friends Don't Let Friends Remain Immature

Mature adults have friends who speak truth into their lives. This is partly because mature people run in packs, like wolves do, and also partly because maturity is shaped by maturity, more than any other single factor. You can watch this basic principle at work in many facets of life. As the saying goes, "If you want to soar with the eagles, you need to quit hanging around with the chickens."

One of my best childhood friends graduated from a Christian university and then went on to become a gifted actor and comedian. We remained close despite living in separate parts of the country, and in the ten years my friend spent dying of cancer, my wife and I were among the tiny inner circle of his caregivers and confidants.

Throughout his life my friend brimmed with social confidence and was a magnet for others. He didn't just walk into a room, he conquered it. Five minutes after meeting him you liked him already. Ten minutes after meeting him you honestly believed he was an old and trusted friend. He charmed everyone that way, and sincerely so.

The youngest of three children, he had two older sisters with these same gifts: verbal, expressive, confident, outgoing, and immediately likeable. It seems highly improbable that any three birth children could be so confident and outgoing, but in fact it's highly probable, given the environment in which my friend was raised.

He had two Christian parents, both of whom stayed around to raise him. His father was a traveling salesman for a church-related publishing company. His mother, among her other ventures, was a successful real-estate agent and steady multilevel marketer. Both were outgoing, highly social, intelligent, witty, humorous, sincerely religious, and entirely self-confident.

Their children turned out the same way, despite differences in sex, personality type, and birth order. There is not a quiet, introspective, nerdy geek among these three, not anywhere—and thus no one this author can relate to on a personal level! But this is not surprising when you consider the nature of the parents.

The combined force of two parents with very similar traits became irresistible (apparently) for three young lives growing up in this kind of home, being shaped by the interaction and correction of two mature adults on a daily, close, intimate basis. Looking back at it now, it appears to be a foregone conclusion that these children would flourish in adulthood.

While my friend's career in comedy, drama, and the entertainment world may have been a unique choice among his siblings, he was prepared for that choice by the environment in which he was raised. His core competencies were formed in his family home.

Where Maturity Comes From: Our Social Settings

This is how maturity forms in persons. It doesn't create itself. Rather, it needs a working model, preferably up-close and readily available for skeptical, unscheduled inspections. Faux maturity rarely fools anyone, even the young. It is not the stuff of our highest aspirations. But genuine maturity, the real thing, is attractive to everyone except the most hard-core of fools.

Maturity forms when immature emerging adults develop close relationships with mature emerging adults. Younger women learn from confident, skilled older women. Younger men learn from strong, gifted older men. Children learn from parents or from the older children in their home. Maturity passes along maturity.

If you are younger among your siblings, do you have any memories of an older brother or sister actually teaching you something, patiently and well? Better yet, did your older brother or sister make you feel like an equal somehow during the process?

If you grew up in a church youth group, was there a time when an older teen seemed to "include you" in his or her inner circle, treating you like a peer? Can you remember how elevating and life-changing that moment was, how validated and affirmed you felt when someone older and wiser connected with you peer to peer?

If you attended school outside the home, was there ever a teacher who didn't seem to "step down" to your level but instead treated you with gentleness and respect, taking the time to be sure you actually learned something? Do you remember the joy of not only gaining knowledge, but also gaining a relationship that somehow felt equal?

This is how maturity forms: A more mature person invests time and energy in a less-mature person, yet does so in a way that isn't condescending. Rather, it is inclusive and democratic and welcoming. (A more mature person who has a condescending attitude is a higher-order moron, the type we call an oxymoron.)

Finding Mature Friends: The Time Is Now

Mature friends help us move in the direction of maturity. One way or another, mature adults bond with other mature adults for purposes that go beyond the social and emotional. They surround themselves with differing wise and outside points of view that can help them eliminate their own blind spots, identify their own weaknesses, and develop their own gifts and potential into their highest and best use.

This is how mature adults develop. It is also how they stay alive and growing. Mature adults thrive in the company of other mature adults, always learning and testing and listening and refining and moving forward.

The lack of this close-in, networked contact with maturity is why so many immature persons remain locked in unproductive and even self-destructive habits, patterns, and career trajectories.

Maturity and Immaturity: It's in the Environment

Lisa and I spent a dozen years doing community development in an inner city. In many ways we were blissfully ignorant when we began the process. Twelve years later we were still blissful but also somewhat better informed. In those years of community life in a crime-filled urban setting, we witnessed all of the social patterns that conspire to keep inner-city residents from becoming mature citizens.

Whether the challenge of the day was gangs or drugs, whether we were providing emergency response to a domestic disturbance (always in the same apartment complexes), or whether we were doing our best to form a cohesive and supportive youth group from among ethnically diverse, dissimilar teens, the consistent patterns could begin to overwhelm us after a while.

Children who grow up being yelled at learn how to yell (profanities).

Children who grow up being beaten learn how to terrorize others.

Children who grow up without a mature adult in their home learn how to be immature, irresponsible, and profoundly unwise even as they get older in years. They may keep on replicating these patterns until they destroy themselves and others, or until their lives are interrupted by the criminal justice system, or intercepted positively by intentional, mature role models with whom they can interact and learn at street level. Lofty theories about social transformation are nice, but local incarnational maturity is better.

Which is why God often guides people to do community development, and why our inner cities in North America are being invaded by an emerging generation that is ready to plant gardens of faith in weedy and waterless places. This we must do, because it is not only the right thing for our society and for our future as a culture, it is also following the contours of God's heart.

God has always cared for the poor and less-privileged.

You can read more about it in His book.

Missing in Action: Mature Examples

In a fair and just world, all of us would have access to mature, self-sacrificing friends. Their presence in our lives would, among other things, help us figure out who to marry, or at least who to marry when we're ready to make that sort of commitment.

Immature friends are of little value in this process. They are jealous of us, or suspicious of our motives, or simply not wise enough to understand what sort of person would be a good match for us as a life partner. Immature friends clutter our lives with trivial pursuits and gossip. Mature friends, even if they are splattering us with paintballs, tend to help us grow up and move forward, helping us birth the real.

If you are thinking about getting married, mature friends are great sources of good counsel. They may come from among your own family members: a wise uncle, a seasoned stepmom, or a distant cousin. You'll recognize maturity when you find it. Mature friends may also come from a small group at church, or your kayaking club, even your network on MySpace, Facebook, or Xanga.

While you're welcome to seek advice from all your friends, including those who are immature, not all advice is created equal. Listening to a mature friend, you'll hear things like how well your personality meshes with another's, how well your common interests synchronize, and what the differences in your family backgrounds might mean. Listening to an immature friend you'll get a lot of feedback about emotions, personal appearance, or the promise of financial stability (which is always an illusion anyway).

Somehow being in the market for a life partner brings out the needy side in most of us, and it's not always pleasant. It's a lot more fun to have our act together, or at least appear to, and let the world come to us for advice. But no matter how wise and smooth we may be in other areas, most of us fumble when we make choices about marriage.

This is where wise friends come in. They help us look at, think through, pray about and, in general, consider the deep things involved in forming a marriage. They help us see ourselves as we really are, not as we imagine ourselves to be. They help us birth the real, look in the mirror with courage, and begin changing the things about ourselves that need to change.

Mature friends help us see things in proper perspective, so we don't spend hours gazing at a reverse image, getting it wrong. Since it's easy to get things wrong, maybe we need to abandon the mirrors (which are broken anyway) and surround ourselves with the wisest, most mature, most spiritual friends we can find.

If we do that, we may discover that we don't "need" to marry. And when we do choose to marry, we may be blessed with a better union because we've learned from those around us. We've made a wise, rational, mature decision instead of a shallow, emotional, stupid mistake.

Just because mistakes are out there doesn't mean we have to be the ones who keep making them. This is why God gives us friends.

⁓

Once we are married, we have access to a 24/7 friend, a friend who is closer than all others, a friend who lives with us and has a good chance to know us as we really are. Ideally we bring our own maturity into this friendship and our partner brings maturity also. This pairing of maturities helps us build a strong relationship that benefits both of us and provides stability for any children in the home.

Together for life, regardless of circumstances and consequences, the two of us can partner together in birthing the real. We can tell each other the truth, always emphasizing the good, the beautiful, and the progress being made. We can admit our own mistakes, which will be many. We can forgive the mistakes of our partner, which may be few.

We will speak well to each other in private; we will speak well about each other in public. Avoiding criticism, sarcasm, and negativism, we will work first on our own shortcomings, rather than judging our partner. Yet we will also steadily, positively tell our partner the truth. Our partner will not only give us permission to do so, but will ask us to do so, invite us to do so, hope that we do so.

In a world of few safe places, marriage is designed to be an oasis of secure love. Satisfied, fulfilled, long-term married couples often tell us their marital paths included hard times, rough places, and all kinds of setbacks. They also tell us that the journey became easier as they grew to know each other, deeply and fully; as their relationships took on TV, the core values of transparency and vulnerability; and as each partner became truly known...and thus truly loved.

The friend you live with has the potential to be the most useful friend you will ever experience. Together with him or her, you can truly become the person you were created to be—the person you have the potential to become if you will patiently, consistently, intentionally do the hard work of growing up and becoming mature.

Having someone do that work with you, helping you achieve it and learn from it, is one of the most lasting and meaningful aspects of being married. You can have access, almost 24/7, to the kind of sounding board and "mirror" that will help you mature, learn, grow, improve, and refine yourself.

The value of that is simply beyond measure.

7

Learning the Dance

This is what single people do:
they try each other on for size.
But everyone's an adjustment.
No one is a perfect fit; there's
no such thing as a perfect...

—Architect Sam Baldwin,
played by Tom Hanks in *Sleepless in Seattle*

Relationships are a difficult dance.

Even when you seem to find your soul mate, even when you appear to fit together like pieces of a jigsaw puzzle, even then...before long you begin to notice some rough edges and some places where the two of you aren't always in synch.

Welcome to the dance.

There's good news, though. Even after a lifetime of flying solo, you can learn to share your home, your finances, and your daily life with another person. You can explore how to care for, gladly serve, and build up another person. You may not win the dance contest—at least not on your first try—but you have a great chance of becoming a finalist and pretty good odds of eventually winning it all. Even if you're new to the dance floor, you can learn some highly effective moves.

~

We get asked about the dance all the time.

Should the man always lead? This question comes to us from

churchgoing, Christian couples before and after they marry. They're trying to sort out what male leadership looks like in a practical way. If a man leads, is he the one who handles the checkbook and manages the family finances? Is he the one who should be more prominent and visible in making everyday decisions? Does he need to be assertive and outgoing while his wife is quiet and reserved? Does he control the discipline of the children and the way they are trained?

Everyone wants to learn how to dance. Some believe there's only one true and right way, and it is critically important to them that they discover this right way and then follow it to the letter. Often, such couples end up frustrated by conflicting advice and competing ideas. Opinions vary, especially on the matter of dancing.

In more conservative churches and settings, a capable and godly woman may want to learn how she should "follow" her husband after living her whole life as a high achiever. She's self-disciplined, intelligent, and talented—now she's wondering how much she's supposed to "stay in the background" as she marries and becomes a wife. What does that look like in real life? What if she's 35 or 40 years old and well along in her career before she accepts this seemingly subservient new role?

A quiet male is drawn to an outgoing and highly competent female. She's good with money, comfortable with making decisions, and the two of them fit together well. Now all of a sudden he's wondering, Does he have to assume "control" of daily issues like finances? If his wife is in control of these matters, will other people (especially within the church) be judging him in some way? Should he avoid marrying this strong and competent female because her abilities may outshine his own?

Welcome to the dance. Nobody said it was easy.

Learning, Growing, and Finding Balance in Scripture

It helps to live a long time and to study marriages and families with keen interest. It helps to go to graduate school. It helps to speak and write and teach and publish. It helps when you attend conferences and retreats and seminars and workshops and are often tasked with being the presenters at these events.

So with the benefit of our more than two decades of careful study and learning, here's a clue about the dance, right up front. Some Christian couples grow and thrive in a relationship where the woman is obviously more gifted in administration and leadership. In these pairings the wife manages the money, makes daily decisions for the household, and is probably seen by others as "leading" in these ways.

> When you follow the pathway marked out by Christ, the dance of marriage becomes not a power struggle but a mutual serving of each other that expresses itself in mutual encouragement.

If you're a couple who fits this category, you can find some useful biblical help in Proverbs chapter 31. If you haven't read the passage lately, check it out. You'll find that the godly woman who is described here is clearly gifted in matters of finance and administration. One of the ways she earns praise is by running her household with shrewdness and skill. Her husband admires her for this accomplishment.

So if you're a couple in which the woman shines in these areas, relax already! There is a clear biblical model for wives managing their households with excellence. These wives earn the praise of their appreciative husbands, who notice their many talents.

Other couples deeply believe that a man's leadership means he is in direct and daily control over issues large and small, including money management, discipline of the children, and all other family matters. Some of these couples have men who are clearly gifted in these areas; some do not. Two decades of careful observation assures us that these couples thrive also, especially when both partners share the same core values and are in agreement about their gifts, roles, and partnership.

The dance is not "one size fits all," even when you adhere very cautiously to scriptural guidelines. This becomes even more true as you gain an understanding of servant leadership, following Christ's model of loving the church. When you follow the pathway marked out by Christ, the dance of marriage becomes not a power struggle but a mutual serving of each other that expresses itself in mutual encouragement.

Often the question is not about who is in charge of a specific area or a process, but whether or not both partners have a voice in these matters. As family counselors, we are always uncomfortable when only one partner has a voice. This isn't a healthy pattern. There are times we decline to perform marriages, when it's obvious that one partner—potential husband or potential wife—is not being heard in the relationship and will not have a useful vote during family "elections." In these cases we advise the couple to start birthing the real before they consider renting a chapel.

It's difficult to say these things to an engaged couple, particularly if they've already set a date and begun planning the ceremony. But if a minister or counselor won't say these things to a couple, who will? The silence of the clergy may be another factor in our high divorce rates. Despite apprehensions and misgivings about how well a couple may be suited for each other, sometimes clergy go ahead with the wedding anyway. Perhaps the parents are significant donors to the congregation. Or perhaps it's just clerical kindness gently manifesting itself. In any event, counselors and ministers, priests and rabbis need to find their courage more often, telling couples, "Wait a while until you know each other better" or, more difficult, "You two are not very well matched."

We've said these things, never comfortably or easily, and we have declined to perform wedding ceremonies or suggested they be significantly delayed. We would rather a couple delay or break off an engagement than marry if they're highly likely to split up, separate, and divorce.

Some couples we meet with choose to listen to our advice and respect it. Some do not. Life is like that—we do not always welcome or recognize wise counsel when we are fortunate enough to receive it.

How We're Wired

Sometimes people fall in love with the idea of marriage—with the idea of being married and having a partner or a family or both. This idea grows stronger and stronger down inside them until they just can't wait.

They find somebody, or someone finds them, and the couple rushes forward. One or both of them are so in love with the idea of being married that they race down the aisle before the flowers wilt. Somehow they believe that the next stage of their life will be wonderful and fulfilling and special. After all, they're getting married!

What could possibly go wrong in the days ahead? Confident that love conquers all, these couples rent a chapel and plan a honeymoon. Before long the chapel is a distant memory and the honeymoon is very much over. Once-loving partners are bickering, growing distant, holding grudges, and yelling angry comments at each other.

Someone should have seen this coming, and perhaps someone did. Yet did the counselor or pastor or parent suggest that the match did not seem wise, that the relationship was yet too young, or that these two adults should simply wait a while, get better acquainted, and then make the wedding plans later rather than sooner?

Someone should have found their voice and said something.

Tales from the Journey of Denial

Big wet snowflakes are drifting down outside and I'm watching their descent through a partially frosted window. I am sprawled out in a booth at a Friendly's restaurant, reading a newspaper while nursing a lukewarm cup of bland coffee. Here in the frosty Northeast, where coffee beans do not grow, coffee is a brown-colored liquid served warm. Once upon a time it was served hot—until someone spilled a hot cup of coffee all over themselves in a drive-through lane. Now it's served lukewarm to warm, sometimes in a printed cup that warns about the dangers of heat. There is no warning about the lack of taste. There should be.

I am waiting for a starry-eyed couple to arrive so we can have their first session of pre-marriage counseling. I do not know them well; I am here as a referral. During the past few years I have married a few of their friends. Their friends must be happy because none of the previous couples has asked me for a refund. (Technically, a refund would be difficult since I don't charge a fee to perform a wedding. I charge nothing at all, and that's often what I'm paid for the counseling, the rehearsal, and the wedding itself.)

The couple is five minutes late, then ten. I check my cell phone—no one has texted me about a delay. So far as I know, all is on schedule.

Fifteen minutes have now gone by, and I wonder if despite our last-minute exchange of e-mails they have somehow forgotten. Then, just as I'm about to call one of them, I see the prospective couple arrive.

They pull into the parking lot at Friendly's in a shiny black BMW coupe. It looks like a 6-series, which has me rethinking my no-fee policy. If this guy can afford to lease a nice BMW, maybe he can also afford to pay a few hundred dollars for pre-marriage counseling, advice about communication and conflict, and a short homily.

The guy jumps out of his car, shuts the door smoothly, and sprints away rapidly while pressing the remote. He's trying to lock his car doors—he'll know it works when he hears the horn honk. But there's no horn honking and the doors aren't locking because his soon-to-be bride is still half-in, half-out of the car, playing with snowflakes. They are landing in her short reddish hair and she has her face upturned, catching snowflakes on the tip of her tongue. She's laughing and sucking big wet snowflakes out of mid-air, and she has a look of joy on her face, absolute joy. I wish I loved cold that much.

The guy, standing by the brightly lit entrance, looks highly annoyed. I can't hear him, but I watch his lips move. I know immediately he is yelling at his future life partner. Clearly he is having a bad day. I have a sudden flash of intuition—I am cursed with it—and I realize this guy probably has a lot of bad days. In fact, most days are bad for him. They must be bad for her too, I surmise.

Our smiley bride-to-be seems unfazed by any of this. She is yelling back at him, but not in anger. I think she wants him to stop and smell the roses by celebrating the snow. But he is in no mood for celebrating. He must know they're already 20 minutes late for their appointment with me.

He yells at her until she quits enjoying the snow, reaches back inside the car for her purse, and eventually finds it. She has barely shut the car door, when the headlights flash and the horn honks. The horn startles her—she jumps. *He might have waited until she was a few steps farther away,* I think to myself. He doesn't seem to be much of a gentleman.

Suddenly I wonder what I'm getting myself into here.

I soon find out.

Beamer (I'm not using real names here, of course) slides into the booth across from me while explaining his tardiness. "Sorry we're late," he insists to me while his tone betrays that he is highly upset. "Elli didn't get ready in time."

Since he's mentioned Elli, I look for her. She arrives four or five steps behind him, smiling. She hasn't heard herself being blamed for their late arrival. "I'm Elli," she says to me, reaching out to shake my hand. "I'm so sorry we're late! It's all my fault."

I smile sincerely at her and try to hold on to that feeling while smiling at Beamer. "No worries," I assure them, a phrase that soon takes on a tinge of irony.

Forty-five minutes into our session, with Elli nursing a small Caesar salad and Beamer devouring a Western omelet, I realize there's no way I'm agreeing to marry this couple on the schedule they are proposing. I won't be ready to marry them in a few weeks, and probably not in a few months either. They are not ready to be married, as many aren't— but beyond that, one of them is completely missing a voice. And the one who's missing a voice doesn't seem to know it.

Ready for the Dance?

Pre-married couples are often the last to know that they're not ready to dance. They don't see it. All they see is a future filled with shopping, cuddling, togetherness, and lots of steamy sex. They'll be joining that big fraternity of married couples (a.k.a. real people) who make up the backbone of our society. Finally, after years as wannabes, they'll become full-on grown-ups. As they think about these possibilities and prospects, they literally can't wait. So they don't.

They flash on a future filled with picture-perfect kids, a great car, some travel, and a smooth house in the suburbs. They'll have a stone fireplace with an oak mantel adorned with lovely framed photographs of their adorable children. They'll have a puppy, maybe a Golden Retreiver or a Chessie.

Pre-married couples, as mentioned, are in love with the idea of being married. And some of them are also in love with each other. That is, they are overwhelmed with a rush of positive emotions, surging hormones, and a growing realization that their world will be a lot less expensive when they quit paying for two homes and two lives, and just pay for one. They are cute—except to their single friends, who secretly resent them for winning the lottery and finally getting a ticket on the train out of loneliness.

We deal with pre-married couples all the time, and we almost always enjoy it. When we don't enjoy it, the typical problem is the one we've been discussing here—one partner doesn't seem to have a voice, and the pairing is unequal from the start. This makes us uncomfortable, and sometimes we are so uncomfortable that we refuse to move forward, except with further counseling. We will not perform a wedding, and we recommend that the couple not get married. We prefer a dose of courage and realism now to the frustration and anger that can result when reality dawns post-chapel, post-ceremony, and post-license. Why not prevent trouble when you can?

Back in the booth at Friendly's, Beamer is giving me a lot of instructions about their service. He doesn't want me to serve communion, he doesn't want a unity candle (waste of time), and he's not very fond of music either. "Wedding singers are the worst," he says while wrinkling his face. "What a great way to screw up an otherwise perfect moment."

We are not here to talk about the service, since I haven't even agreed I will marry this couple. So far I've agreed to meet them and talk about it, which we're doing. But Beamer is rushing ahead, planning the service, making sure I understand that this will not be just another typical, lame wedding ceremony, but a streamlined, efficient, beautiful little event: the perfect wedding in miniature.

Smiley (we are calling her Elli here also, but neither is her real name) is bemused by this but not complaining. After most of Beamer's comments she inserts something like "But I thought we had talked about—" at which point Beamer interrupts her, corrects her wrongheaded thinking, and explains how things actually are. This happens three times before a waiter even arrives to take our order.

It happens once with the waiter at our table. I watch our server raise an eyebrow as Beamer cuts off his intended bride in mid-sentence. "No, honey." He shakes his head as if explaining something terribly simple to a child. "We already talked about this and we agreed that…"

Elli, as if uncertain, nods her head in partial agreement. She manages to smile while doing so. *She is a remarkable person,* I think to myself, *but how long will she keep smiling and nodding her head? Six months? Three years?* I cannot imagine her placidly submitting to Beamer's obsessive control for a lifetime.

At some point in the future, I think to myself while Beamer explains a key facet of his planned reception, *at some point in the future Elli is going to find her own voice.* When that happens, Beamer is going to be one very shocked husband.

Ninety minutes later I agree to meet with them three more times. I would love to be proved wrong in my initial assessment; I would love to discover that there is a deep connection between this couple that will transcend his dominance and the submissive silence with which she responds to him.

In my true heart, I have already decided that it's unlikely I will perform their wedding ceremony. I am wondering if perhaps during our next three counseling sessions I can help Smiley see a way of escape from this stifling and controlling relationship.

In my view she needs one, whether she knows it or not.

Experts on "For Better, for Worse"

Being considered experts on marriage and family issues, Lisa and I are often asked questions about divorce. Most interviewers, whether they are radio hosts or reporters for newspapers, seem to believe they are framing brand-new inquiries.

"Why are there so many divorces today?" is the question I am asked the most.

It took me a while, and several nonstarters, but I've found the answer I like. "Because there are so many marriages," is now my favorite reply.

After my answer, there's usually either a loud laugh or else complete silence in the radio booth. Either response means I was probably heard.

I'm kidding, of course, but on one level it really is that simple. If fewer people got married, fewer couples would get divorced.

Otherwise intelligent and sensible adults get married because they are lonely, because they are happily in like, or because everyone else is doing it. Some of them get married because it's a ticket away from an unhappy home life or dominating parents.

But in general there are way too many marriages happening in our society. Not that marriage is bad—it's wonderful when it functions as God intended. The problem is, people rush forward into marriage before they're ready to learn the dance.

If we set aside spiritual reality for a moment, it becomes easy to understand why couples live together without getting married. From the world's perspective this choice is rational and intelligent. Why should a happy couple contribute to the high divorce rate by becoming yet another statistic? Why clog the courts and flood the legal system with yet another messy disagreement? Isn't it simpler for a couple to just live together and avoid the hassles of making and then breaking their promises?

This is how much of the world thinks, Western Europe and North America especially. But when you carefully think these issues all the way through, living together without making a commitment is just another way of postponing maturity. It's a way of having what you want (sex! pizza! DVDs!) without ever learning to compromise, serve someone else, and become responsible. So although it is possible to see living together as a rational and intelligent decision, ultimately that decision is less mature and less helpful than learning how to make and keep a commitment. It is a virtue to grow up, serve others, and become a responsible, altruistic adult.

Statistics bear this out. Couples that cohabit before marriage actually have worse track records of marital longevity and fulfillment. *Shouldn't it be just the opposite?* most think. But study after study confirms that couples who did not cohabit before marrying end up staying married longer, and enjoying more happiness and contentment within their union.

What's Wrong with Staying Single?

Today's society needs more mature single people: functional, intelligent adults who are beginning to understand themselves. That is, they are beginning to realize how other people see them, and they are beginning to correct their wrong thinking, defuse their defense mechanisms, and learn what they need to know. They are birthing the real before entering a relationship with a life partner.

Good for them! Mature single adults are some of the best things that can happen in a society, and there are far too few of them in today's world. We do have a lot of anxious, permanently depressed single adults who wish they were married—or who believe that marriage, when it happens to them, will transform their otherwise dull and inferior lives into something magical and entirely positive.

We need a society that contains more mature singles, in part because mature singles will marry more wisely if they do choose to do so. I am convinced that having mature single adults in a social system is a great way to prevent divorce, in part because those of us who aren't married can look around and see that there are whole, fulfilled, wise, and wonderful people who are single. We can begin to realize there are other models of health and happiness out there besides coupling.

We can work on growing up first, then figure out marriage later. If we are serious about lowering the divorce rate, this is a very wise approach.

At the end of our fourth session together, I tell Beamer and Smiley that I won't be doing their wedding service. By now I like them (her more than him), and I do my best to sound affirming, positive, and kind as I explain that they're just not ready for marriage.

I graciously attempt to explain my reasoning. "This relationship doesn't have enough of Elli's voice in it," I begin with as much off-handed cheerfulness as I can muster. Then later I talk directly to Elli: "I hope in the days ahead you will speak up more often and let your voice be heard."

We talk about this for a while. More accurately, Beamer refutes my insight at great length while Elli smiles and I nod my head, listening attentively but not agreeing. He instructs her more than once to tell me that she does, indeed, have a voice in their relationship. She follows his instructions without hesitation.

"I do have a voice," Elli insists to me, seeming entirely genuine and sincere. It almost breaks my heart to look at her. She doesn't know what she's missing, and she also doesn't realize that sooner or later she'll figure this out.

Meanwhile, Beamer dictates and Smiley concurs. So simple!

Why am I having a problem with a couple that appears so seamless and smooth in their decision-making and balance of power? Who am I to say that this style of relating is essentially wrong? All I know is, I am profoundly uncomfortable.

After 20 minutes Beamer has not changed my mind. I tell the

couple exactly what I told them half an hour earlier—that they're not ready, that so far their relationship is too one-sided, that Elli's voice is submerged and needs to be fully heard. I say these things as kindly as I can manage, but I am not backing down.

Beamer frowns, perplexed and annoyed. Elli smiles sweetly and assures me she feels fully heard, fully understood in this relationship. Both of them declare that if I won't marry them, someone else will.

I get that. There are ministers on every corner, and justices of the peace waiting in the background if ministers decline. Beyond that, there is always Las Vegas. You can do a quick wedding there and still have time to catch Celine Dion, Barry Manilow, or Wayne Newton at one of the early shows. Anyone who wants to get married can ignore their minister or counselor and find a way to get hitched. It's not that complicated.

Beamer and Smiley go ahead with their plans, and they even invite me to attend their wedding. It feels like a good sign—we're still friends. I didn't mean to judge them, demean them, or offend them by refusing to unite them in holy matrimony. I just wanted them to slow down a little—or a lot—and figure out how to create a mutual, two-person partnership instead of a domineering, one-person dictatorship.

I can be wrong about things, but in the final analysis I have to face one person in my mirror at the end of the day. I need to be able to respect that person, even though I realize how fallible he can be, how stupid at times, how potentially wrong about almost anything.

I would love to be wrong about Beamer and Smiley. I would love that a lot.

Beamer and Smiley stay married less than two years. Then Smiley files for a divorce. When I see her next, she is a stressed-out, harried young divorcee—I have to remind myself I'm talking with the same person. When I see him next, he is quieter and beginning to learn some important things about himself. It will be a slow process.

Will you be repulsed if I tell you divorce can be helpful? Can I say that out loud? I am sad to see the divorce—what other reaction is there? Yet I also realize that two persons are going to begin to grow up here. I only wish their journey growing up had begun while both of them were still single. God help us all.

Divorce—An Unwanted Teacher

God hates divorce, according to a sermon I heard while out of town recently. From the sound of the message, God hates divorced people too. I almost got up and walked out of the sanctuary, but that didn't seem like a holy response. I was close to it, though.

Divorce is a lesson we don't want to learn, coming to us from an unkind teacher. But if we will listen to it, we can learn about ourselves—and learning is good. I know a lot of wise and mature people whose pathway to personal growth began with the last thing they thought they wanted: a divorce.

Some of the most godly and consistent Christians Lisa and I know are ones whose personal journeys have taken them through divorce. While we and they regret this, it is also true that much useful learning and growing has resulted. It is true—there is simply no way around this fact—that they are mature and wise *because* they have gone through a divorce, not in spite of it. So while we wish to avoid divorce always, and while we hope and pray every marriage lasts a lifetime, in the end there is hope if a divorce happens in spite of our best intentions. If we will allow it to be, divorce is a useful and helpful teacher. And most of us have much to learn.

Saying the Difficult Word "No"

If we can learn only one thing as we grow up, maybe it should be how to say no.

We think brides should say no to the proposal, big rock or no rock, regardless of how many family members are gathered around the living room expecting a yes. They should keep saying no until they feel ready—not pressured—to take a partner for life.

We think grooms should say no to pressure from their friends and family, even if they're accused of being commitment-phobes. If you're going to make a commitment, you also ought to hang around for a lifetime and keep it—a decision you should make when you're ready to, and not before.

We think ministers should say no, preferably after several counseling sessions, unless they're convinced the couple is compatible and reasonably ready to form a more perfect union. We think ministers should say no a lot more often, and a lot more kindly, and with a lot of referral resources at the ready—so a couple can move forward and birth the real even though they won't be renting the chapel right away.

We think engaged couples should say no, even standing at the top of the aisle, rather than going through the motions without being absolutely certain it's right for them, the timing is good, and their prospects of bonding for life are reasonably sure and largely positive.

If this sounds like we are encouraging last-minute jitters or amplifying all those normal pre-wedding uncertainties, please forgive us. Everyone has moments of panic when they realize that soon—very soon—their personal independence will end forever. We are not talking here about saying no because you're having an emotional moment. But more to the point, I am also insisting it's not wise to say yes in an emotional moment—which is exactly what too many of us do, every day.

In some cases, just slowing down is going to do a world of good. And in many cases, pre-marriage counseling may be the most helpful gift in the world. There a couple can find an objective listener to facilitate their learning about each other, who can also help them discover who they each are as individuals, helping them learn to do more TV—become transparent and vulnerable with each other and move on toward maturity.

Though we do not consider passing new laws to be the same thing as solving deeply rooted social and spiritual problems, in general we are strong fans of the emerging "get counseling or don't get married" laws that some state legislatures are framing. We happily vote "yes" for that; most marriage and family counselors seem to have the same opinion, tainted perhaps by the fact that it's good for our business.

I have said yes to engaged couples more than 300 times. I have said "no" perhaps a dozen times, maybe two dozen. Looking back, I have never regretted saying the "no." There are several times—I can't give it with a number—that I have later regretted saying the "yes."

Newlyweds for Life

We're at a youth camp, and the entertainment for the evening, after the chapel service wraps up, involves having a "Newlywed Game" with the adult staffers and their spouses on stage as the victims of this process.

It's embarrassing.

Although the questions are simple—favorite color, favorite song, favorite snack food, favorite restaurant—most of the couples are struggling with this. Some have been married only a few years, others a bit longer. There are spiritual questions too: favorite hymn or praise song, favorite book of the Bible, favorite Bible verse.

Couples are bombing out.

The format is simple. With the guys offstage and out of hearing, the women are asked to predict how their husbands will answer. Then the husbands are brought out, asked to answer the same questions, and their answers are compared with the predictions. This happens in reverse also: The wives go offstage and the husbands predict.

All of this is a game-based version of a counseling tool called the Taylor-Johnson Temperament Analysis, which is a more formal way of discovering how well a couple knows each other and how they each predict or describe the other.

The teens are howling. They get no joy at all from correct answers, which are rare and occasional. They get a tremendous kick from the wrong answers, which are many. These couples seem unable to predict what their partners will say, even on the simplest and most basic of questions. Favorite restaurant? Even if you never dine out because you can't afford it, isn't there still a place you'd love to dine at if you could?

One couple, though, is getting every answer right.

Not most answers, but every answer.

The kicker of the evening—the grand finale—is "favorite snack food." It is entirely unclear why this question should be the last one, worth the most points. On the surface it appears to be the easiest. Most people snack, and it's not hard to catch them in the act and notice their indulgence of choice.

The every-answer-right couple nails this one too. "He doesn't eat snacks, but when he does it's got eggs in it. Omelets mostly," says the wife. "I don't know what he'll say, but if he does anything like snacking, it's definitely about breaking some eggs."

Teens laugh. Finally—at last—this couple will get an answer wrong.

The husbands are brought out. Comes the final answer, and the so-far-every-answer-right husband stares at the questioner for a long time.

"Snack food?" the husband repeats, thoughtfully. "I don't really snack. I'm not a candy or cookie or cake or whatever kind of person. But I guess if I did snack, I would probably make myself an omelet. I love omelets!"

Now the teens are screaming. It's impossible! How can this couple get even this answer correct—an answer that makes no sense to anyone in the building?

The truth—although they are not the longest-married or most experienced among the panelists—is that this couple dances. Since the wedding they have been learning, studying new moves, getting better and better acquainted. They are on a nonstop journey to knowing each other and being fully known in return. They are learning the dance—and they're well past the first lessons.

Snack food? Get serious—this couple knows each other, and it shows.

Learning the dance is about stepping outside yourself and

considering the thoughts, needs, wishes, hopes, dreams, feelings, and perspective of another person. This is a stretch for some people, and comes naturally for few. Yet it is absolutely essential if we are going to move forward toward intimacy in a relationship.

Transparent and vulnerable, we allow our partner to know us deeply and truly. Receiving the same blessings from our partner—vulnerability and transparency—we study what we are hearing and seeing. We learn and grow. We gain a whole new way of looking at the world, since now we can see it through our partner's eyes.

That's how TV works. We take the huge risk of being visible as we really are, and in response we become known for who we are at heart. We conquer our fears and open up in transparency to our life partner, and we discover that our partner champions us for being honest and is not afraid to hear about our fears and our mistakes.

TV is scary, but when it works it produces lessons that are infinitely valuable.

It is possible to learn these lessons in a birth family, or in a close friendship, or perhaps in other places. But there is no relationship in the world like the bond between a husband and a wife, committed together for life, who both insist on learning the dance. It is precisely this kind of relationship that provides the protective boundaries within which transparency and vulnerability can do their very best work—for a lifetime.

What mature adults desire—step by step and move by move—is to become fully known by their lover and to fully know their lover in return. With strong passion and with great determination they move forward, not as an obligation but as the greatest adventure they can imagine.

⌒

When you are around a couple who has learned how to dance, you know it.

No one has to announce it to you. You realize, even if you can't explain it, that you're seeing and hearing two people who have an intimate, deep, together-for-life connection—rich, satisfying, and fulfilling. Just being around them makes you hungry. You see what you want for your own journey—a soul-mate marriage.

Although it helps if two persons are compatible, and it's valuable if two persons seek this and find they are a good fit, in the final analysis there are adjustments to be made in every close relationship. There is giving and taking, following and leading.

Out on the dance floor of married life, some people are getting closer, whether or not it was easy as they began. They're doing the work, learning the steps, making the tough decisions to be transparent and vulnerable with each other on a daily basis.

They're dancing.

Can you hear the music?

It's your turn now.

8

Living the Love

I get lonely every time she leaves the room.

—President Ronald Reagan, speaking about wife Nancy

We find our seats at a busy Luby's cafeteria in suburban Dallas.

Across the table from us is an older married couple we haven't seen for a while. She's in her late seventies and he's in his early eighties. They've survived a fairly recent health scare: He had a sudden and severe heart attack. We haven't seen them since.

Visually, they look the same—ageless. Color-coordinated as always, they look like fashion models for an octogenarian magazine. He's Arnold Palmer–tan, his face crinkled into a permanent smile, ready with zingers and one-liners and funny new jokes. She's carefully coiffed and perfectly poised—the epitome of the gracious Southern belle. Like her husband, she can't stop smiling. Also like her husband, she's quick with one-liners, quips, and a fully Christian yet slightly risqué sense of humor.

We don't see them often enough, we immediately realize. If you didn't know their personal history, you would have absolutely no idea that only a few short weeks before he'd been hospitalized and in serious condition.

We're catching up on their lives, munching away on our salads, listening to realistic but upbeat descriptions of his heart attack, treatment, and current medications. Both of them are lighthearted here—if you're picturing relatives who always have to tell you about their latest surgery, you're on the wrong page. We're getting an accurate play-by-play of a serious heart attack and a difficult recovery, yet both husband and wife are positive and smiling as they describe it. They interrupt each other good-naturedly, not to correct one another but to add color commentary to the running narrative.

We aren't quite prepared for this nearly 80-year-old wife to lean across the table toward us at one point, glancing around the cafeteria as if making sure the coast is clear.

"The best thing is," she tells us, lowering her voice to a conspiratorial whisper, "they told us he could go right back to having sex." A wide grin spreads across her face. "So everything's okay in that department. We're right back to normal in that way."

With any other couple, this would be too much information! Much more than we would want or need to know. With this particular couple—one of the healthiest, strongest, and best marriages we've ever observed—the wife's comments cheer and inspire us.

The husband pretends he hasn't heard this brief interlude. "I'm walking every morning now," he tells us. "I had to use the walker at first, but I'm out there in my track shoes again every morning at 7 a.m." He reaches across the table to take the hand of his wife; she grasps his hand tightly and pulls it to her chest.

Life is not a contest. There isn't a "Best Marriage in the Universe" award, at least not on any of our cable channels. Have you seen one? But if there was such an event, the couple across the table from us would be finalists for sure. We've known them up close and personal for all of our lives—they were already old when we were young!—and they genuinely live the love, each and every day.

They dance, and they make the dance look beautiful and inviting.

They inspire us, and on the drive home we celebrate the wife's candid remark about their return to exciting bedroom rituals. We celebrate again once we're home.

~

How many truly great marriages have you seen in your life?

Here's a quick assignment for you, right here and right now. Grab a pen and a piece of paper. Sit down for a minute (not for an hour, just for a minute) and make a quick list of every great marriage you've personally encountered during your lifetime.

Let's be clear: We're talking "great" marriages, not merely good ones. We're not talking about couples who are still together after 20 or 30 years—that's positive, but there's "together," and then there's "great." We're asking you to list only the great unions. Merely good doesn't make the list for this purpose.

Got anything in writing yet?

Don't bother listing any marriages that are shown on television or in films. Those do not count. No great marriages from the world of literature—great or not, most of those are called fiction! What you're counting right now is living, breathing people you've personally known and observed. If you haven't been around them in real life long enough to be sure they're genuine and real, then never mind.

How is your list going? Have you filled a page or two with names of couples? Have you run out of couples to add? Are you done already? Or are you still staring off into space, waiting to begin because you can't think of even one couple that qualifies as having a "great" marriage?

If you've got a list written here's a follow-up question: How much paper did you need for your writing? Did you fill at least one regular-size page with names? Did you just doodle on a Post-it Note? Are you still waiting to think of even *one* couple that fits this description?

Remember, your assignment is to write down the names of couples who are dancing, and dancing well. How's your list coming along?

We often have pre-married couples complete this very assignment during their first or second counseling session with us. The results are fascinating—and also quite consistent over time and across geography and culture. On average, a would-be bride can think of no more than three great marriages. And on average, her intended husband can think of one great marriage at the most. It is not uncommon for both to finally grimace and say, "We can't think of *any* couples like that!"

How does your count compare with these averages from our pre-marriage counseling? If you're a never-married woman, a list of more than four great marriages means either that you're surrounded by an amazing group of family and friends, or else you tend to grade on a curve! Most women compile a list of three or fewer, and one or two is most common.

Men tend to stare at the paper, start to write something down, then stop. Later, perhaps because they believe it's expected of them, they may write down one marriage. So if you're a man with more than one marriage on your list, congratulations! You've just moved to the "above average" portion of our test results.

Women, three or less; men, one or fewer. Do these average scores seem low to you? If so, you wouldn't want to be around during some of our pre-marital counseling sessions as we unpack these lists and talk about the great marriages that two eager-to-be-married adults have personally witnessed. Invariably, at least one couple gets crossed off a list. This couple made the cut for "great marriage" at first blush, but as we talk about greatness and how it functions, the marriage falls off the "great" list and lands somewhere back in the "pretty good" file.

There are a lot of "pretty good" marriages in the world. Let's be sure to celebrate that fact, because it's good news in general. There are a lot of "pretty good" Christian marriages, unions that have stood the test of time and seem to be reasonably okay places. A "pretty good" marriage may not look exciting or "great" to outside observers, but at least it's…pretty good!

The two are still together. Divorce isn't going to happen. They live in the same house, worship at the same church, and hang around together most of the time. They may not laugh very often, but at least no one is yelling or throwing things.

Good for them. Or maybe, pretty good for them.

But is that the goal you're aspiring to, as you think about your own marriage?

How to Move from Pretty Good to Great

We assumed before writing this book that many of you, our readers, would be involved in "pretty good" marriages. We further assumed that if "pretty good" seemed "good enough," then you would not be turning these pages.

So thank you for being unsettled and restless within the context of your pretty good marriage! Thank you for wanting more in your life and in your relationship. Thank you for thinking about becoming soul mates and deciding to move forward in positive directions.

It is usually impossible to grow without being restless.

It is usually impossible to grow without making difficult choices. It is usually impossible to grow without learning how to compromise and make sacrifices.

Yes, great marriages are exceptionally rare. They are also extremely possible.

It's about small-scale servanthood, frequently.

It's about transparency and vulnerability, definitely.

It's about learning to dance.

It's about living the love, daily.

We have a friend who was interviewed for a job as a live-in nanny for a very famous, very public couple. Our friend applied without really believing she had a chance. What she didn't realize is that she fit the mold of what this couple was looking for. (Beyond that, she also has amazing references. We'd trust her with our own young children if we had any, although we'd greatly prefer to raise our kids ourselves.)

Our friend is a single woman, early twenties. She's a high-quality person, and if you wanted to and could afford to hire someone to care for your kids, you would definitely consider hiring her. She's great with children, and her greatness isn't an act or a public posture. It's who she really is, inside and out, to the core. She's a good friend to all who know her, a natural caregiver.

As the process unfolded, she didn't just move forward as a nanny applicant, she actually made it all the way to the finalist category. She was whisked away to a private interview in a limousine that had blacked-out windows, unable to see where she was being taken. This was intentional—for obvious reasons this particular couple keeps their private life as secret as possible in our celebrity-focused, media-intense culture.

Paparazzi hounded the vehicle carrying our friend as it arrived at the gates. Eventually she was actually inside the home, walking through the private spaces, playing in the living room, and interacting with the children of this very famous couple. They wanted to watch as she played with their children—they observed her for several hours as kind of a final test.

Then she was offered the job.

The position paid pretty well, as you might imagine! Yet ultimately our friend did not accept this amazing job offer because doing so would have made her a virtual prisoner within a gated, private compound. She would have little time off duty, and all of her coming and going would be shrouded in secrecy.

She'd be living a 24/7, round-the-clock commitment. And the couple wanted her to sign a multiyear contract, not just agree to a short-term role. This makes sense—wouldn't you want your kids to have some continuity of care as they grew up, especially if you were busy and traveling a lot while your careers arced upward? They were asking a lot of a single young woman. Can you name a dollar figure that makes it worthwhile to give up your entire life?

Our friend struggled with her choice but eventually decided she preferred her freedom and mobility to a life lived in the cradle of Hollywood's arts culture. Her decision made sense to us. In fact, as we talked over her choice on a drive home after visiting her, both of us noticed that we felt relieved, overall.

We'll confess it was extremely interesting to learn about real life in privileged places. And by the way, everything we learned was positive and encouraging to us. If anything, we came away impressed by the private lives of this very public couple.

As we mentioned in an earlier chapter, we also have a friend who has served in child-care roles for a couple who is much less famous but still keeps a high profile. This couple speaks and writes about marriage, and they've been on television screens near you—probably yours. Although our friend is discreet, we did come to learn that there's a "public face" and a "private face" within this couple's marriage. And perhaps things at home are not exactly the way the books make it seem.

Isn't it ironic that you can become an "expert" on a topic and yet not always be able to apply the relevant knowledge and wisdom in your own personal life? Isn't it tragic that your own marriage may exhibit some unhealthy patterns, yet others listen when you prescribe professional advice to married couples?

As Robin Williams remarks in his underrated but compelling little movie called *Father's Day*—"How richly bizarre."

The point of the foregoing? Success in marriage is not about being a great actor or actress, learning how to fake what loving commitment looks like and sounds like. As Abraham Lincoln is said to have observed, "You can fool some of the people all of the time, and all of the people some of the time, but you cannot fool all of the people all of the time."

Faux greatness may fool people for a while, but over time the public posing will be revealed for what it is. Over time the closeness or greatness of your relationship—or the lack of closeness or greatness—will become known to those who know you. It isn't possible to fool all of the people all of the time.

A teen boy went camping with a married couple who are not his parents, and his younger sister came along for the trip also. The couple has served as his lifelong "aunt and uncle"—very close friends of the family though not biological relatives.

The trip involved about two weeks of trekking across Colorado, Utah, and Montana—up hills and down mountains, spending nights outdoors in a large family tent and trapped during the days in a mid-sized SUV, packed beyond overloaded with lots of camping gear, cameras, groceries, and people.

The trip was a lot like real life. It rained at the wrong times, there were black flies as well as red ants around the picnic tables. Although the scenery was idyllic and the trip became highly memorable, real life happened on a daily basis. There were also all of the usual obstacles, setbacks, difficulties, and adventures that happen when suburban families attempt to live outdoors under a scrawny canvas covering for more than a night or two.

Just to make life more interesting, the wife suffers from altitude sickness and gets headaches when she's traveling or living above an 8000-foot elevation. She has to drink lots of water in order to stay healthy.

After two weeks of 24/7 exposure to his aunt and uncle while they were dealing with real life and unexpected situations, the teen came home and gave his parents a candid and unblemished report on the trip. He pulled no punches.

"They *really* love each other," he confided. "I mean, they *really, really* love each other. I haven't seen anything like it," he said, without realizing who he was talking to.

"Also," he added, "they pray about everything. And I do mean *everything!*"

It's hard to fool people on a long vacation, in the rain, when a flat tire happens, day in and day out, living in a tent. If you can fool people for even one full day under those conditions, you should probably switch careers and become an actor. Even so, you probably can't fool people during a two-week-long camping trip—there is too much time, and there are too many ways to become disappointed, upset, surprised, or maybe just plain bored. If you want to find out how people really live out their marriages or their family lives, you should definitely go camping with them.

If you can camp together for a while and remain friends, that's a pretty good sign.

If you can camp together and grow in respect for your friends rather than decreasing in it, that means you've discovered the right kind of friends. Spend more time around them if you can. Maybe they've got something going. As we noted earlier, if you want to soar with the eagles, at some point you have to quit hanging around the barnyard with the chickens. You have to find where the eagles nest, and learn to fly.

Thoughts About Greatness

Greatness in a marriage is about living the love. You can behave with politeness and courtesy, putting on your best self, when you are trying to attract a date or compel a mate. Love is many steps beyond that. You consider someone else before even thinking of your own needs, desires, and wishes. You live out a daily humility and an ongoing sacrifice that puts the wishes and hopes of your partner at a higher level than your own, assigning more importance to helping than to being helped. This is hard work.

What we learn from a marriage is that we like to be served rather than to serve. We prefer being comfortable to getting up off the couch, crossing the room, and making sacrifices to increase the comfort of someone else. At the end of a long day of study, work, or parenting—we just want to relax! And wouldn't it be great if someone else served us for a change? Haven't we been serving and giving all day long?

Human nature screams out, "When is it going to be 'me time' around here?"

Greatness in marriage whispers up close, "It's time for you and what you want."

Greatness in a marriage doesn't think about "me time"—or more accurately, when those kinds of thoughts emerge, greatness takes them captive and serves with even more gladness and consideration.

Taking the Time

It is impossible to achieve greatness in a marriage in just a few years.

As Tom Hanks's character so wisely observed in *Sleepless in Seattle,* "Everyone's an adjustment." We aren't born as a perfect fit with another person. Even in those rare cases where an incredibly compatible couple manages to find each other and marry, there is still a lot of learning, adjusting, growing, changing…and learning again.

Greatness in a marriage can and does happen, it just doesn't happen quickly. No offense—if you've only been married for a few years, we hope you're off to a great start! But let's be clear here, that's what it is. You're off to a great *start.* The odds are strongly against achieving greatness so quickly. If you're ahead of the curve, congratulations—and keep moving forward.

Don't be discouraged by your relative youth and inexperience. As the apostle Paul says to his friend Timothy, "Do not let anyone look down on you because of your youth." Instead, be an example to others of what a godly, excellent marriage looks like in its early stages. As you move toward greatness, keep serving each other and building each other up.

There isn't a signpost along the road or a marker that signals when greatness is achieved. Five years of steadily improving marriage? Probably not enough time. Ten years of steadily improving marriage? Maybe—still seems a bit early. Greatness takes time.

There's no formula. There isn't a number of children you need to raise, nor is it essential that you avoid having children. There isn't an amount of money you need to save.

It's comforting to realize that greatness in a marriage doesn't require financial security, the shallow illusion that many of us chase and that some parents insist on before granting their permission to wed. Financial security? How about this—our treasures are laid up in heaven, waiting for us there.

As we think about it seriously and carefully, we realize that the greatest marriages we've personally observed were households that did not enjoy wealth. It is even accurate to say that these were "poor" couples in terms of money. (Does that mean anything, or is it a statistical anomaly? If we want to pursue greatness in a relationship, do we need to take a vow of poverty, or can we count on it to happen on its own?)

We're standing in the packed aisle of a church in suburban Olathe, Kansas, as the congregation exits from the second morning service. We've spotted one of our favorite couples in the whole world. She sings in the choir, he sits in their regular pew and waits for the choir to be released so she can join him there. He is even capable of sleeping in church: Hardworking farmers do that from time to time. We're pretty sure it's okay with God.

We immediately begin working our way through the crowded sanctuary, hoping we can get to them before they leave. The wife, a spry octogenarian with a warm and engaging smile, sees us coming and points us out to her husband. He gives us an across-the-sanctuary wave. They see us, and they'll wait where they are until we can get there.

We finally get closer. Hugs all around and some general catching-up-on-life follow. The wife is telling us all about her "Sugar Man" and the things he's done for her this past week. He's built things, discovered things, and improved some things around the house. He brought her a mid-morning snack at one point, a treat that was completely unexpected and delightful. She goes on and on with the list—her praises are sincere, up-to-date—and they're all from this past week. Sugar Man is one busy guy!

Sugar Man is uncomfortable with high praise, and he is generally the less verbal of the pair. But when the list ends, he tells us about some baking his wife has been doing—yet another spectacular wedding cake, plus some baking for a church event. He describes her skills in the garden and some things she's been growing, harvesting, and cooking. There is quiet strength and clear conviction in his voice—he adores this woman to whom he's been married for more than half a century.

We're standing in the aisle just soaking up the abundant greatness in this accomplished and lengthy marriage.

This is what greatness looks like and sounds like. No one is pretending here. This still-young eightysomething wife genuinely loves her husband, and that fact is obvious to everyone who knows her. This quiet tower of strength, short in stature but large of heart, truly adores his wife and doesn't mind telling you so.

The marriage they've built together takes our breath away every time we're around it. Needless to say, we're around it as often as humanly possible. Every time, we learn and grow, and we take home new ideas, new courage, and new resolve to keep moving forward with hope and grace, steadily walking toward the sunrise of greatness.

A few years later, we're standing again at almost the same place in the same aisle as this same woman tells us about the loss of her "Sugar Man," who has now gone home to be with Jesus. She is telling us how lonely she is, how much she misses him—we can't imagine!— but she is also telling us that God has taught her how to praise Him in all circumstances, including right now in her season of loss and mourning.

"I am learning to rejoice in the Lord always," she is telling us quietly through tears that are both joy and suffering. It's not a trite phrase she has learned or taught in a Sunday school class. It is a life conviction. Despite her sorrow she is rejoicing in the Lord because, among other things, He granted her an amazing marriage for a very long period of time. Her joy—even right now through her sorrow—is contagious and real.

"I am just so blessed," she assures us as we hug her and express our love.

Two Joys That Come Together and Connect

Greatness in marriage is about growing up. It's about birthing the real, learning the dance, and living the love. Whatever it's about, it isn't about you. It's about God, finding your way to a lifelong partnership with Him. It's about serving the life partner God has granted you, dying to self as you daily sacrifice for her or his good.

Birthing the real is about learning TV. It's about how to be transparent and vulnerable, not with everyone you meet but definitely with the life partner to whom you've pledged forever. Though most of us aren't born being comfortable with vulnerability and we may learn from life that it's not always safe to be transparent, we need to take the risk and birth the real.

Somewhere, with someone, we need to be who we really are, even when we fear rejection, abandonment, or anger. Somewhere, with someone, we need more TV: more transparency, more vulnerability, so we can become fully known. Birthing the real is about moving together in this direction of more TV, more of the time, more often.

Masks will need to melt, walls will need to crumble, and barriers will need to come down. Yet marriage—of all our human relationships—is exactly the place of safety where this kind of openness should be possible for each of us. The fact that marriage often falls short of this goal does not mean we should quit believing in it as an idea.

Learning the dance is also about finally growing up. It's about giving in, making a deliberate sacrifice...choosing to bless your life partner with time away, a brief respite from the daily grind, or a few hours more sleep as you feed the baby or change the diaper in the middle of the night. Which of us naturally desires to do these things? Even a mother's love, one of the strongest loves known on earth, wanes at 2:30 a.m., and especially so when Mom has been up past midnight caring for a sick or unhappy baby. Even a mother's love has its limits, which is why growing up and learning the dance is so vitally important.

It takes two to tango. When only one party gives in and makes sacrifices, the road to greatness is not yet in view. When both parties make sacrifices, deny themselves, and put the needs of their partner ahead of their own—watch out. Here is a couple who is learning to dance; here is a couple who may tango to greatness before your very eyes.

Living the love is letting God's light so shine in your marriage that other people—outside looking in—are dazzled by what they see and hear, what they observe and learn. Living the love is about two people who are committed to transparency and vulnerability in their behind-closed-doors, just-us-two walk together as a couple.

Living the love is about forgetting self, ignoring distractions, and focusing on how to honor God and serve your partner not as duty or obligation, but with a freely released joy that finds its true home in a place of humility and servanthood. Such joy soars; yet when two such joys come together and connect, a fire of greatness ignites and roars. And around such a fire, all of us are warmed and changed.

⁓

Wherever you are on your journey, you're in a great place to start.

Right now is a great time to switch on some TV and get going. Why not try a little transparency before this day is over? And as for vulnerability, how long has it been since you shared a fear or anxiety with your life partner, not trying to sound stronger or braver than you really are, but simply admitting that sometimes you're as frightened as a little child—and you feel exactly as mature and capable.

All of us feel that way, but many of us—especially men—learn to paste on a mask of confidence and competence that hides our true hearts. We aren't nearly as brave or certain or successful as we try to appear. We are cowards at times, easily frightened and even more easily discouraged. We often feel like failures, sometimes even in the midst of what seems to be outward success and triumph.

These things are true for women also. Although women in general seem to come of age being more open and honest about their inner lives, the truth is that they also can learn to wear masks and hide away their inner feelings. This duplicity, even when well motivated, only leads to isolation and being unknown—not a deeper, stronger, closer relationship.

If we are meant to be partners for life, there must be more—much more.

We are meant to find a life partner and come home to a warm

embrace, an encircling heart and hearth where all of our cares and fears can be admitted with freedom and simplicity. Basking in the glow of an unconditional love, we can dare to be who we truly are, and partner with another who dares also.

This is life as we were both to live it.

This is birthing the real, learning the dance, living the love.

This is how to become a soul-mate marriage, starting right here and right now.

Ah, not to be cut off,
not through the slightest partition
shut out from the law of the stars.
The inner—what is it?
If not intensified sky,
hurled through with birds
and deep with the winds of homecoming.

—RAINER MARIA RILKE

More help
for the journey

Your TV Guide

Ideas for channeling greater transparency in your marriage

As you follow the pathway toward more TV—transparency and vulnerability—that we've outlined in this book, you may find that some roadblocks will show up.

After more than two decades of working with married couples, we've heard most of the typical excuses husbands and wives think of when they try to avoid growth. We've learned why some couples end up moving forward successfully toward greater transparency, and why some adults (usually men) resist becoming vulnerable.

Below, we've given some more typical situations and actual cases that illustrate what you may encounter on your journey. May you be one of those couples who works through the difficulties and continues to move your marriage relationship in positive and useful directions!

Why Real Men Won't Get Real

Sunny, age 38, has been married to Jack for almost ten years. They attend one of our retreats featuring the "More TV" theme and then go home to put the basic principles into practice. There's only one problem—Jack won't let himself move in the direction of being vulnerable and transparent.

"That's not who I am," he tells his wife. "I'm just not built that way."

Jack's objection is typical of many men. Men are naturally competitive, and they seem to arrive on Planet Earth hard-wired for conquest and achievement, not sharing feelings.

Ready to go climb a mountain? Real men are with you. Time to storm out onto the football field and beat the opposing team? Real men are there, ready to play. Time to sit down and share what you're deeply afraid of? Sorry—real men won't go there.

Deep down, men desire respect and admiration. Even if their workplace role is menial and their rate of pay is marginal, real men want an arena—somewhere—where someone looks up to them, respects them, and admires them. Real men especially want these things within their marriage and family life.

A man wants to be deeply and truly respected by his wife. He wants his children to look up to him and admire him. He's honored if they follow him into his profession; he enjoys talking with them about what he does, how he does it, and about problems he may have solved while at work.

This explains why a father may teach his daughter basketball. He's not really trying to prepare her for a career in the WNBA—he's just trying to show her something that he, personally, is good at. Being a real man, he doesn't sew, and he's not into the world of fashion. But put a basketball in his hands and he can drive the lane, post up, and score. Real men enjoy showing their daughters—and their wives—how to play basketball, baseball, soccer, and other sports. A wife who is willing to learn these sports, even if she doesn't apply her new knowledge very often, is clearly being the kind of partner that makes a man feel valued, respected, and admired.

Often, it is a perceived lack of respect at home, rather than a sexual itch that needs scratching, that eventually makes a man open to having an affair. He meets a woman who laughs at his jokes, makes him feel popular and even successful—plus, she seems to greatly respect him. Very quickly he is drawn to her and wants to spend time with her. This is even more so when he goes home to a wife who belittles him, complains about him, and wears him down with constant criticism, sarcasm, nagging, and put-downs.

The comparison between the two environments—one of respect and one of ridicule—becomes too hard for the man to ignore. He is aware of it even below the level of his conscious thoughts. He finds himself more and more attached to the woman who shows him a higher level of respect, appreciation, and admiration.

Faced with no respect at home and the appearance of respect somewhere else, men are likely to open themselves to a new relationship, even if they don't initially intend to become sexually unfaithful. Yet even the noblest of roads can lead to the bedroom.

The Vicious Cycle that Prevents Transparency

Men fear transparency because they are afraid of losing respect. If a woman is not already showing active, appreciative respect for her husband, she is unlikely to draw him into a conversation in which he becomes transparent. Men are wary about becoming more vulnerable and revealing because they fear that women will see them as "less than" they were before they admitted something. Men aren't interested in losing; they want to conquer and win.

This frustrates women, many of whom claim they'd respect a man more if he'd just admit his true feelings! The result is a vicious cycle: Wives would respect their husbands if only the husbands would share their true feelings; husbands withhold their true feelings because they are inwardly afraid of losing the respect of their wives.

The best approach? As a wife, make it abundantly clear that you respect your husband and value him as a person and a leader. Watch for small ways to allow him room for transparency. While talking about your kids, try a question like, "Aren't you ever afraid we're failing as parents?" Or, perhaps better, phrase the question like this: "Don't you sometimes wonder if we're raising Emma the right way?"

Obviously, these are not questions to be introduced in the middle of an argument or during a heated discussion about whose parenting ideas are the wisest. Instead, questions like these are best raised when you are already talking about your kids and considering options and approaches in a friendly, cooperative, searching-for-answers way.

The Conqueror's Guiding Rule: Trust No One

Men compete with each other rather than trusting each other. Trust, when it does occur among men, is usually built by long-term shared experiences, such as serving together in the armed forces, playing together on a sports team, or working together on a challenging project on the job.

Men bond by sharing experiences rather than sharing feelings. On a weekend camping trip or a particularly strenuous group hike, men may find ways to express true thoughts, personal fears, or inner worries. These expressions will likely be peripheral to the moment, not the purpose of it—men don't climb rocks to have tea parties.

> Men may become transparent or vulnerable as the result of trust that grows while sharing adversity, travel, or active team sports.

You will usually find a man's closest friends among those with whom he has shared difficult, challenging, or intentional experiences. Men who played football together 30 years ago may, later in life as businessmen, form powerful social networks. More than any other single reason, this happens because they have a pre-existing trust factor that originates from the shared experiences and especially the shared adversity.

Thus, few men are closer than those who serve together in wartime. Those who landed at Normandy, survived the Bataan march, or endured captivity in Vietnam often have lifelong connections that transcend any common factor of personality, capability, or profession. Shared experiences bond such men together and form networks of trust and respect that often endure permanently.

This being true, a backwoods camping trip or a strenuous regimen of jogging or exercising may be a great way for a wife to gradually gain the trust of her husband. By simply being there and sharing experiences with him, she is more likely to hear him voice his thoughts, feelings, fears, and frustrations. These may emerge at the most unlikely times: at the summit of a difficult climb, at a campfire after a long day of whitewater rafting. Men may become transparent or vulnerable as the result of trust that grows while sharing adversity, travel, or active team sports. What you cannot possibly pry out of a man using the strongest crowbar, you may find coming out on its own around a roaring campfire or near a backyard barbecue pit.

Our hero Wesley says it well after an epic battle scene in *The Princess Bride:* "We are men of action." Men are more likely to emote and admit their feelings as a byproduct of their shared experiences and adventures. Men are less likely to emote and share their thoughts over biscotti and a skinny latte.

Men Wonder, *So Who Else Are You Telling About This?*

One couple began to make progress toward mutual vulnerability until the husband learned his wife was sharing intimate details of their conversations with her best friend, another married woman who attended the same church. The two couples spent time together and interacted frequently at church and social events, which meant the husband was now often in the company of a woman who knew his "inner secrets."

Very quickly, the husband quit having "inner secrets"—or at least quit sharing them with his wife. Why would a husband want other women knowing his deepest thoughts, fears, and anxieties? Simply put…he wouldn't.

Married men sometimes learn their wives are sharing private information, such as facts about the couples' sex life, with family members and friends. Usually this type of conversation occurs within a circle of women who already trust each other and who are used to sharing their lives at a deeply intimate level.

When women share facts and revelations about themselves, they are probably on safe ground among family and friends. Yet when they cross the line and begin to share private information gleaned from their husbands or boyfriends, this quickly alienates most men and causes them to flee any type of transparency or vulnerability.

Once again, this issue is rooted in a man's deep desire to be respected. The last thing a man wants to find out is that a bunch of women, perhaps aunts and mothers and sisters and grandmothers, are sitting around discussing, over cups of coffee, his inner worries, his anxiety about a recent job loss, or his personal health problems.

Men may complain about their wives to other men (this is unwise but common), yet most do not share intimate details about their wives in these settings. "Yeah, she's always nagging me about stuff," a man may say to his friends over lunch. He voices this as a complaint, perhaps to gain sympathy. Though men brag and complain and whine, in general they do not reveal secrets about their girlfriends, lovers, or wives. Men intuitively keep such secrets because they want such secrets about themselves to also remain private. For men, secrets are secrets—they are not meant to be shared with others.

Before a man admits something personal and meaningful to a woman, he often asks himself, *Who else might she be telling this stuff to?* If the woman has a pattern of revealing private marriage and family information to other women, her husband is much less likely to suddenly become "an open book" with her and admit his fears and failings.

Men love to have their praises sung within a circle of women, but even the strongest man cringes at the thought that such a group might be aware of his recent failures, deep frustrations, or personal problems. When and if a man does choose to open up to his wife, he is not thinking, *Wow, I sure hope she tells her mom about this.* Instead he is hoping that what he tells his wife in private, remains in private.

What Women Want: Your Attention

Women value thoughts and feelings. Their conversation naturally tends to include these things because they place importance on the life of the heart, on a person's emotions, on the nature and depth of relationships.

Exposed to conversations of this type, men often opt to tune out, pick up the remote control, and avoid "TV" by turning on the television. This sends a clear signal to their wives: *I'm much more interested in Brett Favre's current career choices than I am in learning about your hopes, dreams, and feelings.*

Wives get the message quickly. They tend to withdraw, often nursing a growing feeling of resentment and bitterness at being unloved and unappreciated. For women, this is how affairs may begin. Believing her husband no longer cares or is interested, a woman may gravitate to a man who is a good listener, empathetic and caring.

> Women express what their hearts are feeling and what their minds are processing as a way of bonding with their husbands at heart level.

Note to husbands: If you want to win your wife's admiration and respect, you *must* learn to pay attention to her.

When women begin to share their innermost thoughts and feelings, some men naturally want to become teachers. "That makes no sense at all!" a man may exclaim, apparently believing that all of life is a schoolroom and that he has the chalk. Such men appear to believe that the purpose of life is teaching and communicating objective truth in a clear manner so their wives can learn the facts.

As if!

"Only a complete idiot would believe that!" another man exclaims to his wife. In so doing he does reveal the presence of a complete idiot: himself. When we teach the process of communication in marriage, we call this unhelpful pattern *invalidation*.

Invalidation is the process of negating or attacking a person's feelings, rather than being open to hearing how another person thinks, feels, or believes. It ought to be safe for any of us, husband or wife, to express our personal feelings.

Most wives do not, in general, voice thoughts and feelings as a way of initiating a classroom discussion about philosophy, science, or religion. Instead, women express what their hearts are feeling and what their minds are processing as a way of bonding with their husbands at heart level. These expressions of feelings are open-ended and are not meant as "final answers" to life's great questions. They are intended as a way of building closer personal intimacy rather than a way of doing educational homework.

Women who seek rational answers and professorial tutoring will usually ask for such things. More likely, they'll go back to school and enroll in some new classes. They'll be great students, and they'll be quite clear in their pursuit of education in a formal and official way. They'll respect an instructor, and they'll bring their best student-selves to the classroom.

Meanwhile, when a wife brings up a feeling or an idea at home, she is usually not asking to be reprimanded, analyzed, informed, advised, or lectured by her husband. When she brings up a thought in casual conversation, most of the time this reflects a normal adult tendency to wonder, inquire, seek, and learn from experience.

Wives process their thoughts and feelings in the company of their husbands as a way of showing their mates that they are valued and cherished. Men who tune out these conversations not only miss the point, they make a powerful counterpoint: *Your feelings don't matter to me, at least not during football season and particularly not during* Monday Night Football!

This is not the kind of message that builds great relationships. While women are wise to learn good timing and appropriate moments for conversation, men would be wise to figure out their own inner core values—building a fantastic marriage relationship or becoming even more of a couch potato than they already are.

Repeated note to husbands: If you want to win your wife's admiration and respect—and win her heart—you *must* learn to pay attention to her.

Moving Beyond the Excuses

As we mentioned earlier, in two decades of counseling married couples, listening to them closely and speaking to them frequently, we've heard pretty much every excuse there is. Happily, we've also watched some couples "catch fire" and decide to chase after a strong marriage the way a young Michael Jordan or Larry Bird one day decided to "play basketball."

When a married couple starts passionately, intentionally, actively pursuing a closer and more meaningful relationship, they create an unstoppable force. They begin to build a momentum that overcomes obstacles, ignores excuses, and forges ahead with power—and usually with success. When they do hit a bump in the road, such couples keep right on going. They may slow down for a bit, but their direction doesn't change—they are moving forward, going on toward greatness, chasing the marriage of their dreams.

Such couples move from *having* dreams to *living* them, from wishing they had a stronger union to actually having the kind of union other couples wish for. (Such couples are the ones you put down on your list of truly great marriages in chapter 8.)

We're blessed to know some, and we mention a number of them in the acknowledgments and the dedication of this book. We mention others in some of the chapters here. And there are more, unlisted (so far), whom we hope to mention in our future writings.

Most of all, whether we know you personally or not, we hope the two of you reading this book are just such a couple—a present or future "success story" who will inspire the marriages around you to do more TV, to build a more perfect union, and to remain together for life in a loving, sharing, unselfish, and other-focused relationship.

If you're on that journey today…no matter how early in the process or how far down the road you are…we salute you. May you meet with much success, and may the grace and mercy of God surprise you with good things along your route.

Guide for Thought and Discussion

*Questions to help you discover more about
your relationship and take action to move forward*

We have designed these questions to give you, or you and your partner together, the opportunity to dig deeper into three key chapters of our book. (If you do it together, you'll have a chance to begin "learning the dance"!)

We've also provided space if you wish to write down your answers or make some notes on what you're finding out about you and your partner. We pray that these next few pages will take you forward in your journey to a soul-mate marriage.

Chapter 1: "Chasing the Magic"

1. How transparent are you in your relationship with your mate? Using a scale where 100 percent is "fully transparent," what is your percentage of transparency with your partner? Write your score below.

2. Have you experienced circumstances or surprises that led to greater levels of transparency on your part? Have there been times where

you didn't really intend to disclose so much about yourself, yet somehow everything just "came out"? Describe one of these times.

3. In what ways do you reveal and disclose personal and private things to your life partner? How often do you do this? Does your life partner hear about your fears, worries, setbacks, struggles, and temptations? To what extent are you honest and open if these topics emerge when talking with your spouse?

4. Are you able to talk to your partner candidly about your most embarrassing moments and the times you felt like a failure? Have you shared with your partner in this way? How did he or she respond? What happened when you shared this kind of intimate feeling or emotion or situation with him or her?

5. Do you find yourself avoiding intimacy and avoiding honesty, and pretending to be wiser, more successful, or holier than you really are? Why or why not? Is there any other living person (not including your spouse) who knows the real you? If so, why?

6. If you have a choice between guarding yourself emotionally and becoming more open and vulnerable emotionally, which do you usually choose? Why do you make this choice? Under what conditions might it be safe for you to become more open, more self-revealing, more honest, and more vulnerable?

7. Can your spouse trust you to keep his or her secrets? Will you guard private information and keep it between you and your partner? Or do you have a pattern of sharing intimate and revealing details with friends and family? If you do have such a pattern, are you willing to make significant and permanent changes in the amount and nature of information you share with others?

8. Do you respect people more when you don't actually know them… or when you watch them go through a trial or difficulty, trying and perhaps failing, yet honestly and openly admitting their struggles? Why do you respect those who don't try to hide their true feelings?

Chapter Two: "Melting the Masks"

1. What news stories have you heard lately in which a person was

214 — The SOUL-MATE *Marriage*

suddenly caught living, or discovered to be living, a life much different than his or her life appeared to be? Was this person a pastor, a politician, or some other public figure? Why do you think the story received as much public attention as it did?

2. Why do you think some people choose to live a secret life in addition to their obvious and evident public life? Do you believe that most people do this, or is it abnormal and atypical for someone to behave in this way?

3. Did you conceal any of your personal traits while you were dating your spouse—before the two of you got married? Did you try to appear neater, gentler, smarter, or otherwise different from what you really are? Did these efforts succeed somewhat, or did your true character slip out and become visible before you eventually married?

4. Are there habits, attractions, temptations, or problem areas in your life that you are currently concealing from other people, including your spouse? Do you understand and believe that God "sees us in secret" and thus knows all about these habits, attractions, or addictions?

5. What addictions or habits or struggles do you need to begin confessing as soon as possible to your spouse or perhaps to others? What patterns do you need to begin breaking so they no longer have power over you? In what ways can you begin giving God new levels of control over your life and your identity?

6. Does a church in your area, or perhaps your own church, offer a ministry, such as "Celebrate Recovery," that helps people overcome codependency, anger, drug and alcohol issues, and sexual addictions? (If you are unaware of these kinds of resources, do a web search under "Celebrate Recovery" to find local chapters.) Are you willing to consider attending such a group?

7. Have you ever thought or realized how many adults—people just like you—struggle with some kind of addiction, negative pattern, or unhelpful behavior? Are you aware that getting help begins by simply admitting that you do have a problem?

8. How soon can you sit down with a counselor, a pastor, or a trusted friend and begin to identify the areas of your life that need changing? How soon can you begin making an action plan for meaningful change?

Chapter Eight: "Living the Love"

1. As this chapter suggests, sit down for a few minutes and make a list of the truly great marriages you have personally observed. Remember—marriages from film, TV, romance novels, and so on, do not count. These need to be real-life couples you have personally seen and observed. List the great marriages in the space below. Do you need more space for your list?

2. As you think about the great marriages on your list, what are some of the common traits shared by these unions? In the space below, write down two or three similarities or common traits these marriages share.

3. How do you think these marriages achieved these qualities? Do you think this kind of greatness just happens or is a matter of luck? If not, what did these couples do to become so close, so strong, so unified? What do these couples already know that you are still learning at this stage in your life?

4. How can your marriage move forward toward this kind of greatness? Do you think greatness in marriage can be achieved quickly,

or is it more likely to emerge over a longer period of time? Can you see yourself having a great marriage two or three years from now? Ten years from now? Twenty years from now? Can you see your kids and grandkids celebrating your marriage as one of the "great ones" on their own lists?

5. Write down two or three practical ways you could serve and help your spouse right now, during his or her typical or normal week. When can you start doing this kind of serving? How soon do you think your new behavior will start making a difference?

6. Write down two or three ways you can begin building up your spouse, helping him or her be more confident or feel more successful as a person, partner, parent, or in some other role. How can you begin to affirm your partner in these ways? Is your partner more likely to "hear you" if you write a note, send a text message, whisper something during pillow talk, or in some other way?

Take the "greatness pledge" with your partner. Over coffee or a meal, sit down and write a note that pledges that from this day forward the two of you are on a journey toward greatness in marriage. Both of you sign and date your pledge. Better yet, show it to some friends and family members so they can keep you accountable for growing closer and stronger in your union.

Acknowledgments

How do we first learn the truth about love and marriage?

For most of us this learning begins within our families of origin. We observe and listen to the daily interaction of our parents or grandparents, stepparents or guardians as they raise us and care for us. We watch them and listen to them, and we begin to form our understanding of what married life is about.

Although we've thanked each of these four persons in some of our other books, this new book is a wonderful place to again give thanks to Lamont and Ruth Jacobson, Lisa's parents, for being such excellent role models of Christian married life during their 59 years together, as of this writing. This book is also an excellent opportunity to thank Lee and Marilyn Frisbie, David's parents, married for 57 years as of this writing, for so consistently showing us what godly marriages look like and sound like. For Mom and Dad and Mom and Dad, we are forever grateful: We are still learning many good lessons from all four of you! As we celebrate our thirtieth anniversary while writing this new book, we are hoping to one day match your records for marital longevity. God is good!

Early in our married life we attended a vibrant, growing campus church that was led by Dr. Paul Cunningham. We learned so much from his teaching, from his stories, and from his own powerful personal example. Meanwhile his gracious wife, Dr. Connie Cunningham, taught a weekly Sunday school class for young married couples like us. We are still drawing upon a flowing wellspring of ideas, concepts, and strategies that Connie taught us in her class. Our own marriage and our teaching about marriage have been permanently impacted for the better by the two Drs. Cunningham. Their wisdom and insight continue to bless us; through their speaking and writing both of the Cunninghams keep blessing others also.

The two of us met, grew past infatuation into serious love, and committed our lives together while we were students at MidAmerica Nazarene

University. Like so many other campus settings, MNU provided a place for God-seekers to meet each other, attend worship and praise together, serve side-by-side in ministry together, and become friends.

For each of us, our time at MidAmerica was spiritually and personally formative. We sat in chapel services, especially the annual Valentine's Day chapels but also many others, in which Dr. Gerard Reed delivered witty, insightful, extremely well-crafted messages about relationships and God's design for them. Gerard had our full attention in those chapels—we were definitely interested in the topic of relationships! Meanwhile Gerard and his wife, Roberta, modeled for us the kind of marriage we hoped to achieve someday, full of grace and creativity, high energy and obvious mutual affection. While we are working on this book we've received the news that Roberta has left Gerard's side in order to be with Christ in heaven. Our thoughts and prayers are with our good friend Gerard.

Arthur and Mattie Uphaus modeled abiding love and beautiful romance in the "senior years" of their lives. Mattie taught us several courses in creative writing; yet any class from Mattie was a lesson in spiritual formation and personal growth. Her contagious enthusiasm for all of God's works—and for each one of God's children—transformed our understanding of Christian involvement in the arts. As we began to hone our writing skills and be published, Mattie was our most energetic cheerleader! She was already in her mid-eighties by then, yet no one could cheer more loudly or smile more brightly. We look forward to seeing her again in our eternal home.

Professor Gertrude Taylor exemplified a loving support for her husband while teaching us so many valuable lessons about prayer, trusting God, and spiritual growth. While our attention was focused on the spiritual lessons, Gertrude constantly showed us how a godly wife cheers for, encourages, and blesses her husband. Later, during graduate study at another school, we had occasion to learn from her husband, Dr. Mendel Taylor. Both of these gifted Taylors impacted our lives with the wisdom of their teaching and also by the power of their personal examples.

Sprinkled throughout the campus of MNU were married couples with various roles in teaching or student life or administration or landscaping or the physical plant. Regardless of their places of service, these couples were visible to us almost constantly: We watched them interact with each other, with the students, and with us. We learned from their words and from their examples. Among many we should mention we include Rolland and Margaret Gilliland, and Dr. Hardy and Lucille Weathers. Thank you for teaching us about marriage even when you didn't realize we were studying your lives!

We will never wonder whether or not we should each have attended MNU. Instead, we will spend every day that God gives us being grateful for the many blessings of that campus and those who served it, plus now the lifelong friends we've gained from among our peers at MidAmerica. Although our guaranteed student loans are paid in full, we cannot repay our true debt to the university. We return as often as possible; so far David has attended every commencement exercise since the school's first, in 1972. It's a tradition we hope to continue for as long as we both shall live!

For now the fourth consecutive time the gifted team at Harvest House Publishers has blessed us with sage advice, timely counsel, creative cover art, page design, proofreading, editing, and more as we've launched a new book project. Among many team members, Terry Glaspey is a wise and godly mentor for whom we are deeply grateful; Terry's vibrant gifts as a presenter, word-crafter, mentor, and editor continually reflect the light and love of Christ in ways that compel and inspire us on our journey. Paul Gossard is a peer-acknowledged editor whose commitment to excellence and remarkable word-crafting skills refine our raw material and improve it greatly from its original state. So to Paul and Terry, to Carolyn and Barb, to Dave and Sharon, and to the many others we interact with at Harvest House in Eugene, Oregon: Thank you! We are blessed to be included among the Harvest House family of authors.

Resources for Growth in Your Marriage

Family Centers, Organizations, and Resources

Association of Marriage and Family Ministries

Primarily a network of speakers, writers, and counselors working in issues related to marriage and family. Web site provides links to many helpful resources; this organization also sponsors an annual conference for workers in family ministry.

Web address: *www.amfmonline.com*

Center for Marriage and Family Studies

An educational center focused on helping families adjust to trauma and change, especially after divorce, separation, or abandonment. Four primary areas of study: 1) Divorce Recovery; 2) Single Parenting; 3) Remarriage; and 4) Blended Family (Stepfamily) topics, issues, and challenges. Speaking, teaching, and consulting.

Directors: Dr. David Frisbie and Lisa Frisbie

Web address: *www.MarriageStudies.com*

Crown Financial Ministries

Teaching, training, and numerous resources in Christian financial principles, helping families and others manage financial resources according to biblical wisdom and prudent stewardship. Among founders: Larry Burkett (d. 2003).

Web address: *www.crown.org*

Family Life

Speaking, teaching, and special events for couples and families from a Christian perspective, including conferences and seminars. Schedule of upcoming programs and events listed on website. Among principals: Dennis Rainey.

Web address: *www.familylife.com*

Focus on the Family

A global ministry organization devoted to strengthening the family through broadcasting, publishing, speaking, and equipping. Produces and publishes numerous resources for many aspects of family life; some materials are available at no cost upon inquiry. Many other resources available for purchase or as gifts with donation to the ongoing ministry. Founder: Dr. James Dobson.

Web address: *www.family.org*

Getting Remarried

A wealth of helpful information related to the preparation and planning of a remarriage, as well as helping remarried couples with all aspects of family life.

Web address: *www.gettingremarried.com*

Instep Ministries

Programs, resources, and support for single, divorced, and remarried persons from a Christian perspective. Focus on reconciliation, restoration, healing, and hope.

Directors: Jeff and Judi Parziale.

Web address: *www.instepministries.com*

Institute for Family Research and Education

Resources and materials for families, including blended families and remarriages.

Directors: Dr. Donald Partridge and Jenetha Partridge.

Web address: *www.ifre.org*

Ronald Blue & Company

Christian financial management services, currently with over 5,000 clients and managing over $3 billion US dollars in assets. Focus on biblical principles and effective stewardship from a Christian perspective. Founder: Ron Blue.

Web address: *www.ronblue.com*

Smalley Relationship Center

Teaching, speaking, and publishing resources for couples and families. Books, conferences, events at locations nationwide. Founder: Dr. Gary Smalley.

Web address: *www.dnaofrelationships.com*

Stepfamily Association of America

Publishes *Your Stepfamily* magazine. Provides education and support for persons in stepfamilies and for professionals in family therapy. Numerous helpful resources and programs, many with local availability and access.

Web address: *www.saafamilies.org*

Successful Stepfamilies

Teaching, training, speaking, and publishing materials for stepfamilies providing wisdom from a caring Christian perspective. Conferences at various locations.

Numerous helpful links to other related organizations on the Web site. President: Ron L. Deal.

Web address: *www.SuccessfulStepfamilies.com*

Counseling, Professional Referrals

National Association of Social Workers

The National Association of Social Workers maintains a network of social service providers in each state, organized through state chapters of the NASW. By making contact with the chapter in your state, you can obtain information about providers of counseling and other social services in your city or region.

The NASW Web site maintains a database of information, services, resources, and members which can guide you to locally available providers.

Web address: *www.naswdc.org*

Information regarding the address and phone number of each state chapter is listed below in alphabetical order.

ALABAMA
2921 Marty Lane #G
Montgomery, AL 36116
(334) 288-2633

ALASKA
4220 Resurrection Drive
Anchorage, AK 99504
(907) 332-6279

ARIZONA
610 W. Broadway #116
Tempe, AZ 85282
(480) 968-4595

ARKANSAS
1123 S. University, Suite 1010
Little Rock, AR 72204
(501) 663-0658

CALIFORNIA
1016 23rd Street
Sacramento, CA 95816
(916) 442-4565

COLORADO
6000 E. Evans, Building 1,
    Suite 121
Denver, CO 80222
(303) 753-8890

CONNECTICUT
2139 Silas Deane Highway,
    Suite 205
Rocky Hill, CT 06067
(860) 257-8066

DELAWARE
3301 Green Street
Claymont, DE 19703
(302) 792-0356

FLORIDA
345 S. Magnolia Drive,
    Suite 14 B
Tallahassee, FL 32301
(850) 224-2400

GEORGIA
3070 Presidential Drive,
 Suite 226
Atlanta, GA 30340
(770) 234-0567

HAWAII
680 Iwilei Road, Suite 665
Honolulu, HI 96817
(808) 521-1787

IDAHO
P.O. Box 7393
Boise, ID 83707
(208) 343-2752

ILLINOIS
180 N. Michigan Avenue,
 Suite 400
Chicago, IL 60601
(312) 236-8308

INDIANA
1100 W. 42nd Street, Suite 375
Indianapolis, IN 46208
(317) 923-9878

IOWA
4211 Grand Avenue, Level 3
Des Moines, IA 50312
(515) 277-1117

KANSAS
Jayhawk Towers
700 S.W. Jackson Street, Suite 801
Topeka, KS 66603-3740
(785) 354-4804

KENTUCKY
310 St. Clair Street, Suite 104
Frankfort, KY 40601
(270) 223-0245

LOUISIANA
700 N. 10th Street, Suite 200
Baton Rouge, LA 70802
(225) 346-5035

MAINE
222 Water Street
Hallowell, ME 04347
(207) 622-7592

MARYLAND
5710 Executive Drive
Baltimore, MD 21228
(410) 788-1066

MASSACHUSETTS
14 Beacon Street, Suite 409
Boston, MA 02108-3741
(617) 227-9635

MICHIGAN
741 N. Cedar Street, Suite 100
Lansing, MI 48906
(517) 487-1548

MINNESOTA
1885 W. University Avenue,
 Suite 340
St. Paul, MN 55104
(651) 293-1935

MISSISSIPPI
P.O. Box 4228
Jackson, MS 39216
(601) 981-8359

MISSOURI
Parkade Center, Suite 138
601 Business Loop 70 West
Columbia, MO 65203
(573) 874-6140

MONTANA
25 S. Ewing, Suite 406
Helena, MT 59601
(406) 449-6208

NEBRASKA
P.O. Box 83732
Lincoln, NE 68501
(402) 477-7344

NEVADA
1515 E. Flamingo Road, Suite 158
Las Vegas, NV 89119
(702) 791-5872

NEW HAMPSHIRE
c/o New Hampshire Association
  of the Blind
25 Walker Street
Concord, NH 03301
(603) 224-4039

NEW JERSEY
2 Quarterbridge Plaza
Hamilton, NJ 08619
(609) 584-5686

NEW MEXICO
1503 University Boulevard N.E.
Albuquerque, NM 87102
(505) 247-2336

NEW YORK
New York City Chapter
50 Broadway, 10th Floor
New York, NY 10004
(212) 668-0050

New York State Chapter
188 Washington Avenue
Albany, NY 12210
(518) 463-4741

NORTH CAROLINA
P.O. Box 27582
Raleigh, NC 27611-7581
(919) 828-9650

NORTH DAKOTA
P.O. Box 1775
Bismarck, ND 58502-1775
(701) 223-4161

OHIO
118 E. Main Street,
  Suite 3 West
Columbus, OH 43215
(614) 461-4484

OKLAHOMA
116 East Sheridan, Suite 210
Oklahoma City, OK 73104-2419
(405) 239-7017

OREGON
7688 SW Capitol Highway
Portland, OR 97219
(503) 452-8420

PENNSYLVANIA
1337 N. Front Street
Harrisburg, PA 17102
(717) 758-3588

RHODE ISLAND
260 West Exchange Street
Providence, RI 02903
(401) 274-4940

SOUTH CAROLINA
P.O. Box 5008
Columbia, SC 29250
(803) 256-8406

SOUTH DAKOTA
1000 N. West Avenue #360
Spearfish, SD 57783
(605) 339-9104

TENNESSEE
1808 W. End Avenue
Nashville, TN 37203
(615) 321-5095

TEXAS
810 W. 11th Street
Austin, TX 78701
(512) 474-1454

UTAH
University of Utah GSSW,
   Room 229
359 S. 1500 East
Salt Lake City, UT 84112-0260
(800) 888-6279

VERMONT
P.O. Box 1348
Montpelier, VT 05601
(802) 223-1713

VIRGINIA
1506 Staples Mill Road
Richmond, VA 23230
(804) 204-1339

WASHINGTON
2366 Eastlake Avenue East,
   Room 203
Seattle, WA 98102
(206) 322-4344

WEST VIRGINIA
1608 Virginia Street E.
Charleston, WV 25311
(304) 345-6279

WISCONSIN
16 N. Carroll Street, Suite 220
Madison, WI 53703
(608) 257-6334

WYOMING
P.O. Box 701
Cheyenne, WY 82003
(307) 634-2118

About the Authors

Authors of ten books and dozens of articles about marriage and family life, Dr. David and Lisa Frisbie serve as executive directors of The Center for Marriage and Family Studies. The Center's primary focus is helping families adapt to crisis and transition, with special attention to postdivorce family dynamics: single parenting, divorce recovery, remarriage issues, and stepfamily/blended family life.

The Center also maintains an active interest in serving clergy marriages and families, as well as military marriages and families. Dr. and Mrs. Frisbie speak at retreats and conferences for clergy and spouses and have been instrumental in developing weekend retreats and ongoing curriculum for both teen PKs (pastor's kids) and also TCKs/MKs (third-culture kids, missionary kids). They serve military couples and families as crisis counselors with such issues as re-entry and postdeployment homecoming and readjustment.

Traveling frequently to speak, teach, and train has taken David and Lisa to all 50 of the United States, 11 of Canada's provinces, and more than 30 nations of the world to date. In addition to his background in marriage and family counseling, Dr. David Frisbie is an ordained minister who has performed more than 300 weddings in diverse locations and across boundaries of culture and language.

David and Lisa are frequent contributors to *ParentLife* magazine (Lifeway, Southern Baptist Convention) and have been named and quoted in *USA Today* and the *New York Times* among other print outlets. Their broadcast media appearances include ABC-TV and CBS Radio in addition to numerous local television and radio stations. They have been interviewed by Chuck Bentley of *MoneyLife* (Crown Ministries) and by Jim Burns for his popular radio broadcast *HomeWord*.

Previous books by Dr. and Mrs. Frisbie have been selected as "Recommended Resources" by Willow Creek Community Church, Focus on the Family, Concerned Women for America, Billy Graham's Bookstore at the Cove, and numerous other organizations and ministries. Their writing has won many awards and endorsements.

Dr. David Frisbie serves as an adjunct faculty member at Southern

Nazarene University, where he teaches Family Studies and Gerontology in the graduate and professional degree program. Topics of his courses include family dynamics and structure, including divorce and remarriage, single parenting, and issues of aging.

Married for 30 years, David and Lisa teach, speak, and write as a team. While it is often David who carries the bulk of the presenting duties, Lisa is active in researching, editing, and refining the content of their books, seminars, articles, and workshops. By long established practice and strong personal preference, they travel and serve together.

- To inquire about book signings and author appearances, contact **Laurie Tomlinson, Laurie@keymgc.com**

- To inquire about booking the authors for speaking engagements, contact
  Lisa Douglas, mountainmediagroup@yahoo.com

- The authors maintain a writing blog here:
  www.emergingintofaith.blogspot.com

- The Center for Marriage and Family Studies has a Web site here:
  www.MarriageStudies.com

- To contact the Frisbies directly via e-mail, reach them here:
  Director@MarriageStudies.com

Also by David and Lisa Frisbie

HAPPILY REMARRIED

Making Decisions Together • Blending Families Successfully
• Building a Love That Will Last

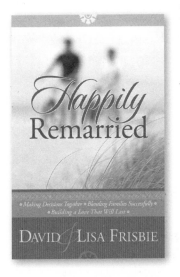

What Can You Do to Beat the Odds?

In North America today, nearly 60 percent of remarriages end in divorce. In *Happily Remarried,* you'll find ways to build the long-term unity that will keep your relationship from becoming just another statistic.

From more than 20 years of speaking, teaching, and counseling, David and Lisa Frisbie understand the situations you face every day. Using many examples drawn from real-life remarriages, they speak with hope and humor about the challenges, leading you through...

- *four key strategies:* forgiving everyone, having a "forever" mind-set, using conflict to get better acquainted, and forming a spiritual connection around God
- *practical marriage-saving advice* on where to live, discipline styles, kids and their feelings, "ex's," and finances
- *questions for discussion and thought* that will help you talk through and think over how the book's advice can apply to *your* circumstances

Combined with the indispensable ingredient of Scripture-based counsel and a helpful discussion guide, all of this makes for a great how-to recipe for a successful, happy remarriage.

To read a sample chapter of this or any other Harvest House book,
go to www.harvesthousepublishers.com

MOVING FORWARD AFTER DIVORCE

Practical Steps to
Healing Your Hurts • Finding Fresh Perspective
• Managing Your New Life

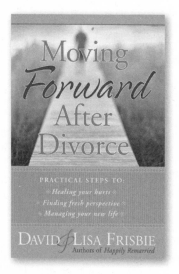

Is There Any Hope on Your Horizon?

More than 2 million Americans experience divorce each year...but you may feel like you're the only one going through it. After such a painful and even shattering experience, how can you start to move forward?

Authors David and Lisa Frisbie have spent more than 25 years learning from divorced persons. Here they offer the best strategies they've discovered—positive, encouraging ideas that will help you...

- raise healthy, mature children, even if you must do it yourself
- develop interests, dreams, and skills into new career opportunities
- find the friends you need to survive this difficult journey
- discover God's role in this new phase of your life
- understand your emotions and move toward healing and wholeness

Real conversations and real-life stories reveal clear, simple pictures of achievable steps—steps that will lead you toward new hope and new possibilities for your future. *Includes questions for growth and reflection.*

To read a sample chapter of this or any other Harvest House book,
go to www.harvesthousepublishers.com

RAISING GREAT KIDS ON YOUR OWN

A Guide and Companion for Every Single Parent

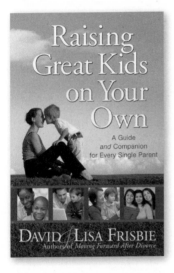

**Good Family—
Great Kids—
You Can Do It, Even on Your Own!**

Raising kids on your own is hard work. Deep down, you may be unsure whether you have what it takes, and whether you're making the best choices to help your kids' future.

In two decades as family counselors, David and Lisa Frisbie have talked to hundreds of single moms and dads. They know what you're going through, and they provide practical and proactive ideas you can use to...

- guide your kids through the hurt and pain that follow divorce
- take care of yourself so you can take care of your children
- build strong connections with family and friends and find support through them
- manage your household confidently as you take on new roles and tasks
- make good decisions about work, education, and relationships

In *Raising Great Kids on Your Own*, effective strategies come to life through the Frisbies' candid conversations with moms and dads who parent alone. Their stories—true stories of the good and the bad, of hope and encouragement—will help you raise your kids with optimism and confidence.

*To read a sample chapter of this or any other Harvest House book,
go to www.harvesthousepublishers.com*

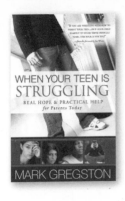

When Your Teen Is Struggling
Real Hope and Practical Help for Parents Today
Mark Gregston

When you've tried everything you know to do, Mark Gregston offers this encouragement: *Don't lose hope.* From his 30-plus years of working with troubled teens, Mark shows you how to help kids work through their pain so they can enjoy the lives God created them to live. With this comprehensive guide, you can...

- develop a belief system your family can live by
- deal with the real issues causing your teens' troublesome behavior
- build healthy family relationships even in difficult times

Mark shares his secrets to survival and success in raising teenagers, offering parents a hand as they struggle for help. As a parent myself, I say it's about time!

—STEVE LARGENT

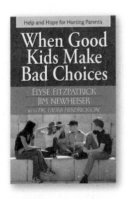

When Good Kids Make Bad Choices
Help and Hope for Hurting Parents
Elyse Fitzpatrick and Jim Newheiser, with Dr. Laura Hendrickson

What are parents to do when a much-loved child makes bad choices? Authors Jim Newheiser and Elyse Fitzpatrick speak from years of personal experience as both parents and biblical counselors about how hurting parents can deal with the emotional trauma that results when a child goes astray. They offer concrete hope and encouragement along with positive steps parents can take even in the most negative situations.

Helpful advice from Dr. Laura Hendrickson regarding drugs commonly prescribed to problem children—along with suggested questions parents can ask pediatricians about behavioral medications—round out this compassionate and practical guide for parents.